Cordon Bleu

Winter Puddings

Cordon Bleu

Winter Puddings

CBC / B.P.C. Publishing Ltd.

Published by
B.P.C. Publishing Ltd.,
St. Giles House, 49 / 50 Poland Street,
London W1A 2LG

© B.P.C. Publishing Ltd., 1971

Designed by Melvyn Kyte
Printed by Proost, Turnhout, Belgium

These recipes have been adapted from the Cordon Bleu Cookery Course
published by Purnell in association with the Cordon Bleu Cookery School
Principal : Rosemary Hume ; Co-Principal : Muriel Downes
Quantities given are for 4 servings.
Spoon measures are level unless otherwise stated ; use plain flour unless
other types are specified.

Contents

Introduction

Winter — when the family are extra hungry because of the cold, and guests are prepared to linger over a well prepared meal. This is the time to use your imagination preparing rich, interesting and satisfying desserts to round off your meals. There is little fresh fruit available, so experiment with pastries, puddings, soufflés and pancakes, gâteaux and creams. If you prefer a cold dessert, there are plenty of delicious seasonal meringues and jelly recipes.

For the current book in the Cordon Bleu series, we have selected some of our favourite winter dessert recipes. The bulk of the recipes are either French or English, but the inclusion of recipes from North and South America, Canada, Germany, Scandinavia, Austria, Russia and the Basque region makes for a truly international selection. As one might expect in a book of winter recipes, the colder countries are particularly well represented.

Cordon Bleu cooking methods are basically French, and the French don't take short cuts in the kitchen. With many of the desserts in this book, particularly pastry and soufflé recipes, the techniques of preparation are very important. We have therefore taken care to give you as many useful hints as possible, as well as the individual recipes. However delicious the recipe, the dish will be spoiled if you make your pastry in too warm conditions, or leave a hot soufflé standing in the kitchen while a guest lights up an untimely cigarette.

In our appendix, we have also included a glossary of some of the special cooking terms used and notes on the preparation of various items that recur throughout the book. Experienced cooks may not need to use this, but if there is anything you do not understand in a recipe, you will probably find it further explained in the appendix.

We have enormously enjoyed preparing this book. There is a certain luxury about sweet foods, unmatched by meat dishes or savouries. We hope you will have as much fun cooking from this book, and consuming the results, as we have had devising the recipes and testing them out for you.

Rosemary Hume
Muriel Downes

7

Pies and tarts

Pie crusts are like promises, made to be broken. Good pastry is often the mark of a good cook, and so many delicious desserts are made with pastry, that it is important to be able to make it well.

Traditionally, an English fruit pie is made in a dish with a lid of pastry on top. The pie is left plain rather than decorated, this is a custom dating from the days when meat and fruit pies were baked in the same oven. The meat pies were highly ornamented and the fruit pies were left plain to distinguish them.

The word tart is often used instead of pie, but correctly a tart is open, with pastry underneath and the fruit or filling on top.

A plate pie is different again — with pastry on top and underneath. These are best made with a firm fruit such as apples, gooseberries or blackcurrants, and should be stood on a hot baking sheet in the oven in order to cook the pastry underneath.

English pastry is traditionally made with butter or a mixture of butter and another fat. This gives it its characteristic rich flavour. Americans normally do not use butter, but shortening. This alters the flavour, and since American flour is milled from hard wheat which is very high in gluten (the major part of the protein content of wheat flour, which gives it its elasticity), and absorbs more liquid than English flour, the texture is very short. It is possible to achieve the short, melt-in-the-mouth texture of American pie pastry with an anglicised version of a traditional recipe.

Good pastry is not difficult to make if certain rules — which are often forgotten — are followed. The main points are :

1 Work in a cool, airy room. Plan to make pastry before the kitchen becomes warm from other cooking because a damp atmosphere is disastrous.

2 Use fresh, fine-sifted plain flour (self-raising flour or baking powder produces spongy textured pastry), firm but not hard fat (hard fat would not blend properly with the flour) and

9

ice-cold water for mixing. Baking powder is sometimes used to lighten a rich pastry that has a lot of fat, or for economy reasons when less fat is being used. If baking powder is used without much fat the pastry must be eaten freshly baked.

3 Handle flour and fat lightly but firmly. When rubbing fat into the flour, keep lifting it up and crumbling the mixture between your fingers. This movement helps to aerate the pastry. Shake the bowl after 1-2 minutes to bring the larger lumps of fat to the surface and to show you how much more rubbing-in is necessary. This is especially helpful when making rich shortcrust, where over-rubbing makes the pastry greasy.

4 Make sure that the correct amount of water is added. This may vary a little with the quality of the flour. Too dry a mixture makes the pastry difficult to handle; it will crack when rolled out and crumble after baking and will be dry to eat. Too wet a dough will shrink and lose shape while baking, and also makes for tough, hard pastry. The amount of water is usually indicated in a recipe and it is important that at least two-thirds of the given quantity is added to the dry ingredients before mixing begins. This avoids over-working and brings the ingredients quickly to a firm, smooth pastry, especially when making the foundation dough for puff pastry.

5 A marble slab or slate shelf is ideal for rolling out pastry because it is smooth, solid and cool; otherwise, keep a board especially for this purpose (a laminated plastic surface is cool). Once pastry is rolled out, always scrape slab or board thoroughly before rolling out new pastry to remove any dough that may have stuck and which might cause further sticking. (This applies particularly to flaky or puff pastry when rolling out is of paramount importance.) Use a minimum amount of flour for dusting when rolling, otherwise too much will go into the pastry and spoil it. A heavy, plain wooden rolling pin without handles is best, especially for puff pastry.

6 Chill made pastry for about 30 minutes or leave it aside in a cool place for the same amount of time. This gives it a chance to relax and removes any elasticity which may cause shrinkage round edge of dish.

7 It is essential when baking pastry to pre-set the oven to the required temperature. The immediate heat sets the pastry in its correct shape and makes it possible to control the exact amount of cooking time.

Note: when terms such as 8 oz quantity of pastry are used, this means the amount obtained by using 8 oz flour, not 8 oz prepared dough. As a quantity guide, 8 oz shortcrust pastry will cover a 9-inch long pie dish holding $1\frac{1}{2}$ lb fruit, or line an 8-inch flan ring. For a covered plate pie (8-9 inches in diameter), 10 oz shortcrust pastry would be required.

Almond fruit flan

For almond pastry
8 oz flour
4 oz caster sugar
4 oz butter
3 egg yolks
2-3 drops of almond essence
4 oz ground almonds

For filling
mixture of fresh fruit in season
  such as pears, grapes, pineapple,
  bananas, strawberries, green-
  gages, etc.
apricot glaze
whipped cream (for serving)

10-inch diameter flan ring

To make apricot glaze :
Put 5 tablespoons apricot jam
and 1-2 tablespoons water in a
pan and warm gently to dissolve
jam, pour through a wire strainer,
return to pan and boil gently
until clear.

Method
Sift the flour on to a board or
slab. Make a well in the centre,
put in the sugar, butter, yolks
and flavouring and sprinkle the
ground almonds on the flour.
Work ingredients together and
chill for 1 hour.

Roll out the pastry, line in to
the flan ring and bake blind in
a pre-set oven at 375°F or
Mark 5 for 20-25 minutes.

Remove the flan ring and,
while the flan is still warm,
brush the inside with apricot
glaze and leave until cold and
set. This will prevent the juices
from the fruit spoiling the pastry.

Prepare the various fruits and
arrange in the prepared flan
case. Brush again with the hot
apricot glaze. Serve with a bowl
of whipped cream.

Upside-down apple tart

1 lb cooking apples (peeled,
   cored and thinly sliced)
2 oz butter
4 tablespoons granulated sugar
8 oz quantity of puff pastry (see
   page 115)

To serve
½ pint double cream (whipped)

Method
Set the oven at 350°F or Mark 4.
Put the butter, apples and sugar
into a round ovenproof dish.
Cook in the pre-set moderate
oven for about 30 minutes until
the apples are barely done.

Remove dish from oven and
then turn the heat up to 425-
450°F or Mark 7-8. Roll the
pastry and cover the dish ; put
it back into the oven for 12-15
minutes. Take out and turn
upside-down on to a serving
dish. Serve immediately with
whipped cream.

Mincemeat flan de luxe

For rich shortcrust pastry
8 oz plain flour
salt
4 oz butter
2 oz lard
1 dessertspoon caster sugar
1 egg yolk
2-3 tablespoons water

For fresh mincemeat
8 oz Cox's apples (weight
   when peeled and cored) —
   chopped
1 oz orange candied peel
   (chopped)
8 oz raisins
8 oz currants
4 oz sultanas
6 oz grapes (peeled and pipped)
2 rounded tablespoons almonds
   (blanched and shredded) —
   see opposite
grated rind and juice of 1 small
   lemon
pinch of mixed spice
6 oz brown sugar
1 oz melted butter
1 small glass brandy, or sherry

To decorate
2-3 tablespoons whipped cream
little rum, or brandy

*8-inch diameter flan ring ; 3-inch
   diameter plain cutter*

Only half this quantity of mincemeat is needed to fill the 8-inch
flan ring. The remainder will
keep up to 2 weeks in sealed
jars (see method).

Method

To prepare pastry : sift the flour
and salt together, cut butter and
lard into flour until well coated
and in small pieces. Rub in fats
until mixture resembles fine
breadcrumbs. Stir in sugar, mix
egg yolk and water, add to the
dry ingredients and mix quickly
to a firm dough.

Knead pastry lightly on a
floured board until smooth.
Chill slightly before use.

To prepare mincemeat : dried
fruit should be washed and dried,
candied peel well soaked in
water to soften. Chop apples and
candied peel separately, then
mix with the other ingredients.
If the grapes are large, cut them
into 2-3 pieces.

When mincemeat is well mixed
set aside quantity to be used
immediately and fill remainder
into jars. Cover with circle of
greaseproof paper and cello-
phane, then tie down or secure
with an elastic band.

Grease and flour the flan ring,
set on a baking sheet. Set oven
at 375°F or Mark 5.

Use three-quarters of the pastry
to line the flan ring. Fill with
mincemeat. Roll out the remaining pastry and cut a circle
the same size as the flan ring.
Stamp out a hole in the middle
with a plain cutter. Put this
pastry ring on top of the flan,
crimp round the edge to decorate and seal in, brush with
water and sprinkle with caster
sugar. Bake in the pre-set oven
for 30-40 minutes.

Just before serving pile 2-3
tablespoons of whipped cream,
lightly flavoured with rum or
brandy, in the middle of the flan.

To blanch and shred almonds :
pour boiling water over the
shelled nuts, cover the pan and
leave until cool. Then the skins
can be easily removed.

Drain, rinse in cold water, then
press skins off with fingers.
Rinse, dry thoroughly, split in
two and cut each half lengthways in fine pieces.

*After lining flan ring with three-
quarters of the pastry, the mincemeat is spooned in. A hole is cut
out of the middle of the remaining
pastry, which is then laid over top
of flan ; edges are crimped to seal*

13

Flan d'Antilles

For French flan pastry
   (pâté sucrée)
6 oz plain flour
pinch of salt
3 oz caster sugar
3 oz butter
2-3 drops of vanilla essence
3 egg yolks

For filling
8-10 sugar lumps
2 large oranges
4-5 ripe bananas
½ pint double cream

8-inch diameter flan ring

Method

Sift the flour with the salt on to a marble slab or pastry board, make a well in the centre and put in the sugar, butter, vanilla essence and egg yolks. Work up together with the fingers of one hand, then draw in the flour and knead lightly until smooth. Chill for at least 1 hour, then roll out, line into the flan ring and bake blind.

Meanwhile, rub the sugar lumps over the orange rinds until they are well soaked with the oil. Crush them and add enough orange juice to make a syrup. Slice the bananas, moisten them with a little of the syrup and fill the flan case with them. Whip the cream lightly and add the rest of the orange syrup to it. Spread the cream thickly over the bananas and serve.

To make French flan pastry, sugar, butter and egg yolks are worked together; then flour is drawn in to make a firm dough

To complete the flan d'Antilles, the pastry case is filled with bananas in orange syrup and covered with whipped double cream

The completed flan d'Antilles

Cinnamon tart (Tarte cannelle)

¾ lb fresh, or canned, blackcurrants
3-4 tablespoons granulated
sugar (to sweeten)
caster sugar (for dusting)
arrowroot (for thickening
canned juice)

For French flan pastry
6 oz plain flour
3 oz butter
3 oz caster sugar
3 egg yolks
1 dessertspoon ground
cinnamon

7-8 inch diameter flan ring

Method
Make up the pastry (see page
14), sieving the cinnamon with
the flour. Leave it for at least
1 hour in a cold place.

Meanwhile pick over the
currants, put them into a large
pan with the granulated sugar.
Stir them over a low heat and,
once the juice begins to run,
cook blackcurrants more rapidly,
stirring frequently, until they are
thick and rich-looking. Turn
them on to a plate to cool.

Set the oven at 400°F or
Mark 6. Roll out the pastry and
line on to flan ring. Push sides
of the pastry well up, prick the
bottom with a fork and chill
slightly. Fill flan with blackcurrants when they are cold.

Roll out the pastry trimmings
and cut into strips; lay these
over the top, lattice-fashion.
Put another strip around the
edge of the flan ring, pressing it
down firmly. Brush the pastry
lightly with water and dust flan
with caster sugar. If canned
fruit is used, thicken some of the
juice with arrowroot. This can
then be brushed over the cooled
fruit in place of the dry glaze.

Bake filled flan in the pre-
set oven for 25-30 minutes in
all; after 10 minutes decrease
the heat to 375°F or Mark 5.
Continue to cook for 15-20
minutes. Serve the flan while it
is still warm. The French call
this 'chambré' (at room temperature).

Beauceronne tart

For rich shortcrust pastry
6 oz plain flour
pinch of salt
4½ oz butter
1 egg yolk
1 rounded dessertspoon sugar
2 tablespoons cold water
whipped cream (optional)

For filling
8 oz curd cheese
2 oz butter
2 rounded tablespoons caster sugar
2 rounded tablespoons raisins
2 tablespoons double cream
3 eggs (separated)
2 tablespoons plain flour

8-inch diameter flan ring, or sandwich tin

Method

Make rich shortcrust pastry: sift the flour with a pinch of salt into a mixing bowl. Drop in the butter and cut it into the flour until the small pieces are well coated. Then rub them in with the fingertips until the mixture looks like fine breadcrumbs. Stir in the sugar, mix egg yolk with water, tip into the fat and flour and mix quickly with a palette knife to a firm dough.

Turn on to a floured board and knead lightly until smooth. If possible, chill in refrigerator (wrapped in greaseproof paper, a polythene bag or foil) for 30 minutes before using.

Line the pastry on to the flan ring.

Now sieve the cheese and work well in a warm bowl. This will help the cheese to absorb the butter, sugar, cream and yolks without curdling, and allow the whisked egg whites to be folded in easily.

Cream the butter with the sugar in a bowl and beat well. Stir in the raisins, cream and egg yolks. When well mixed, whip egg whites stiffly and, using a metal spoon, fold into the mixture with the flour.

Turn into the pastry case and bake for 35-40 minutes in an oven at 375-400°F or Mark 5-6. When cooked leave to cool as the filling rises a lot during cooking and must be left to subside before attempting to remove the flan ring or turn the tart out of the tin.

Serve cold and, for a special occasion, with lightly whipped cream.

Pears 'en douillon'

4-6 ripe dessert pears
2 tablespoons granulated sugar
2 tablespoons brandy
1 egg (beaten)
6 tablespoons redcurrant jelly
1-inch piece of angelica (cut in
   strips)

For rough puff pastry
12 oz plain flour
pinch of salt
9 oz firm butter or margarine
$\frac{3}{8}$ pint ice-cold water (to mix)

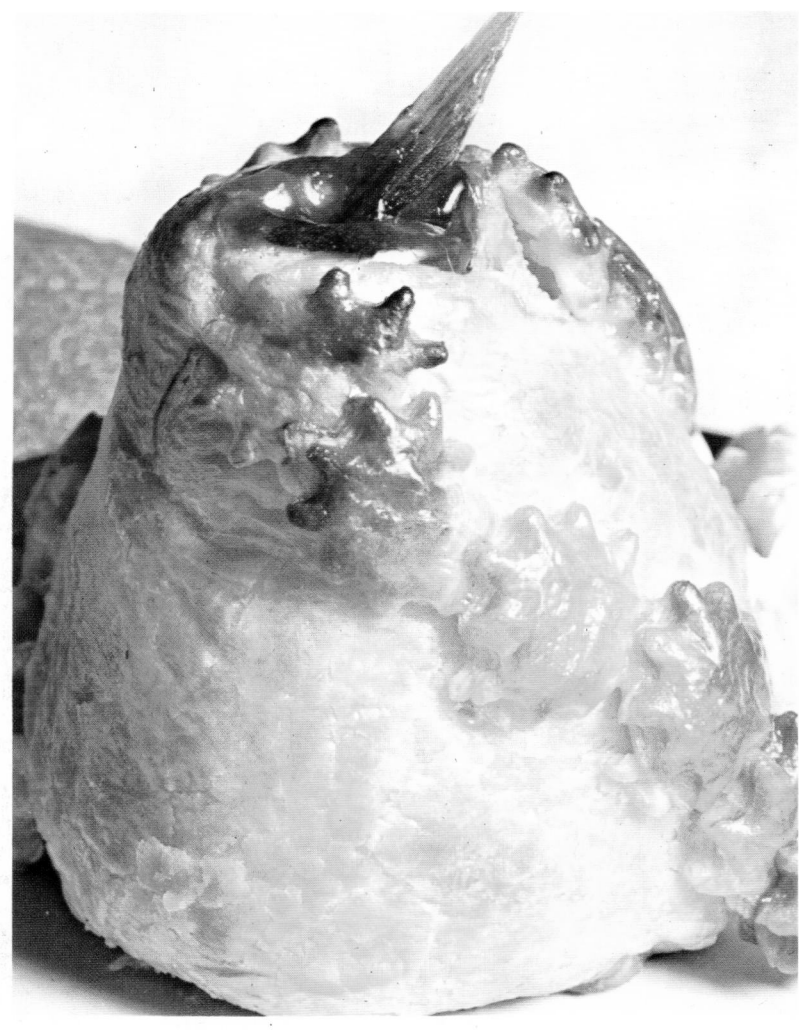

Method

To make pastry sift the flour with salt into a mixing bowl. Cut the fat in even-size pieces about the size of walnuts and drop into the flour. Mix quickly with the water (to prevent overworking dough so that it becomes starchy) and turn on to a lightly-floured board.

Complete the following action three times; roll to an oblong, fold in three and make a half-turn to bring the open edges in front of you so that the pastry has three turns in all. Chill for 10 minutes and give an extra roll and fold if it looks at all streaky, then use as required.

Roll out pastry fairly thinly and cut into squares, each large enough to enclose one pear. Set the oven at 425°F or Mark 7.

Peel the pears, remove the stalk and hollow the centre to remove the core very carefully; do not cut right through the pear. Fill the hole with sugar and brandy. Turn each square of pastry over, then, keeping pear upright, shape pastry around each one. Brush them with beaten egg, leave a hole at the top and decorate with a few bands or fancy shapes cut from pastry trimmings and brush again with egg. Bake upright in the pre-set hot oven for about 15-20 minutes until the pastry is golden-brown and crisp.

Meanwhile beat the redcurrant jelly until smooth and runny, rub through a strainer into a small pan and heat gently. Pour a little warm redcurrant jelly into each pear and put a piece of angelica in the top to resemble a stalk. Serve with a bowl of whipped cream.

Keeping pears upright when wrapping prevents brandy running out

Le poirat (Pear tart)

2-3 William pears
caster sugar (for dusting)
2½ fl oz double cream (lightly
 whipped)

For French flan pastry
8 oz flour
2 teaspoons ground cinnamon
2 oz shelled walnut kernels
 (finely chopped)
5 oz butter
4 oz caster sugar
2-3 drops of vanilla essence
1 egg
1 tablespoon water

Deep 7-8 inch diameter flan ring

Method

Set oven at 375-400°F, or Mark 5-6. Make up the pastry (see method, page 14, adding water with butter, sugar and egg yolks to dry ingredients) working the cinnamon and walnuts with the flour, and put in a cool place for about an hour.

Peel, core and quarter pears. Take two-thirds of pastry, roll it out and line the flan ring. Roll out the remaining pastry and form a round to cover the top; cut a round about $2\frac{1}{2}$ inches in diameter out of the centre of this. Fill the tart with the pears, cover with the pastry ring, brush with water and dust with sugar. Bake in pre-set moderate to hot oven for 30-40 minutes.

Serve warm or cold. Just before serving, pour the whipped cream into the centre of the tart.

American pumpkin pie

For shortcrust pastry
8 oz self-raising flour
pinch of salt
5 oz shortening (Spry or Trex)
about 5 tablespoons cold water

For filling
$\frac{1}{2}$ lb mashed cooked pumpkin
4 oz soft brown sugar
pinch of salt
1 teaspoon ground cinnamon
$\frac{1}{2}$ teaspoon ground ginger
$\frac{1}{4}$ teaspoon ground nutmeg
2 eggs
$\frac{1}{2}$ pint creamy milk

Deep 8-inch diameter pie plate

This is a traditional American recipe.

Method

Make shortcrust pastry : sift the flour with a pinch of salt into a mixing bowl. Cut the fat into the flour with a round-bladed knife and, as soon as the pieces are well coated with flour, rub in with the fingertips until the mixture looks like fine breadcrumbs.

Make a well in the centre, add the water (reserving about 1 tablespoon) and mix quickly with a knife. Press together with the fingers, adding the extra water, if necessary, to give a firm dough.

Turn on to a floured board, knead pastry lightly until smooth. Chill in refrigerator (wrapped in greaseproof paper, a polythene bag, or foil) for 30 minutes before using.

Set oven at 375°F or Mark 5. Line the pie plate. The edge of the pie should be high and fluted and to do this, line the sides and top edge of the plate with two layers of pastry. Press these together firmly and chill well while preparing the filling, then flute or crimp the edge with two fingers and a thumb.

To prepare filling : mix the sugar, salt and spices together. Beat the eggs and stir in the milk and mashed pumpkin. Add the sugar and spices to the pumpkin mixture and pour into the uncooked pastry case.

Bake in the pre-set oven for 45-50 minutes, or until a knife inserted in the filling comes out clean. Leave pie to cool a little before serving.

Watchpoint If using an oven-proof glass pie plate or a tin made of bright metal, bottom heat is required to get the best results. To get this, place a baking sheet in the oven while it is heating and place your pie plate on this for baking.

To cook pumpkin
You will need about 1 lb raw pumpkin to make $\frac{1}{2}$ lb cooked. Peel the pumpkin, cut it up, removing seeds, and stew gently in a little water until tender (about 15 minutes). Strain and mash ; use as required.

Tarte aux pommes grillée

4 oz quantity puff, or rough puff,
   pastry, or 6 oz (in weight)
   trimmings (see page 115, or
   method, page 19)
1 lb (4-6) Cox's Pippin apples
3 tablespoons sugar
½ pint water
2 tablespoons good apricot jam
icing sugar (for dusting)
1 small carton (2½ fl oz) double
   cream (whipped) — for serving

8½-inch diameter pie plate

Method

Dissolve the sugar in the water to make a syrup; boil for 2 minutes, then add jam and stir until dissolved. Peel, quarter and core the apples. Put them in the syrup, cover pan and bring to the boil. Poach gently for 20-25 minutes, then draw pan aside and leave covered until cold, by which time the apples should be translucent.

Set oven at 425°F or Mark 7. Turn apples into the pie plate. Roll out pastry, cut and press a thick border round the edge of plate. Cut $\frac{1}{2}$-inch strips from the rest of the pastry, and lay these over the apples, lattice-wise. These strips can be twisted if wished. Dust with icing sugar and bake the tart in pre - set oven for 15-20 minutes. Serve cold with whipped double cream.

Twisting a strip of pastry before arranging lattice-wise over apples

Lemon cheese tart

1 packet (8 oz) wheatmeal
  biscuits
1 oz caster sugar
2 oz butter (melted)

For filling
8 oz Philadelphia cream cheese
4 oz lemon curd
3 egg yolks

8-inch diameter flan ring, or pie plate

Method

Crush the biscuits with a rolling pin and mix with the sugar in a bowl. Pour on the melted butter and mix in. Reserve one-third of the crumb mixture; press the rest into the flan ring (or pie plate) and chill well.

Set the oven at 350°F or Mark 4. Mix the cream cheese and lemon curd together; stir and add the egg yolks. Pour the mixture into the chilled pastry shell. Sprinkle with the reserved crumbs and bake for 20 minutes in the pre-set oven.

Allow to cool and chill again before serving.

Lemon curd

To make 1 lb lemon curd, put 8 oz caster sugar, 4 oz unsalted butter, the grated rind and strained juice of 2 large lemons and 3 well - beaten eggs into an enamel pan (or stone jam jar) standing in boiling water. Stir gently over low heat until mixture is thick (do not let it boil or it will curdle), then pour immediately into clean, dry jars and cover tightly. Lemon curd will keep for several weeks and should be stored in a cool place.

Apple flan ménagère

For rich shortcrust pastry
6 oz plain flour
pinch of salt
3 oz butter
1 oz shortening
1 rounded dessertspoon caster
   sugar
1 egg yolk
1-2 tablespoons cold water

For filling
4-5 even-size cooking apples
caster sugar
apricot glaze

7-inch diameter shallow flan ring

Ménagère means in the style of the housewife — homely — and this flan is one of the simplest and quickest to make.

It should be made in the shallow French flan ring, as if the layer of apples is too thick too much juice runs, making the bottom pastry soft. For this reason only the top layer of apple is dusted with sugar.

Method
Make the rich shortcrust pastry (see method, page 17) and line it onto the flan ring; pinch round the edge to decorate and chill for 10-15 minutes.

Peel and slice the apples thinly and arrange at once in the flan, making sure that the top layer is neatly arranged in a circle. Dust with caster sugar and bake for 25-30 minutes in an oven at 375-400°F or Mark 5-6, allowing apples to colour. Remove the ring and brush the flan with hot apricot glaze (see page 11).

Norfolk treacle tart

For shortcrust pastry
8 oz plain flour
4 oz butter
2 oz shortening
water (to mix)

For filling
$\frac{1}{2}$ lb golden syrup
2 tablespoons black treacle
1 oz butter
little grated lemon rind
2 small eggs (well beaten)
3 tablespoons cream, or
   evaporated milk

8-inch diameter flan ring

Method
First make the shortcrust pastry and chill it for about 30 minutes (see method, page 21). Then roll it out and line the flan ring; bake blind.

Gently warm the syrup, then add the black treacle; remove from the heat and add the butter in small pieces. When butter is quite melted, add the lemon rind, beaten eggs and cream (or evaporated milk). Mix thoroughly and pour into the pastry case. Return to the oven (set at 350°F or Mark 4) and continue cooking, on the middle shelf, until the filling is set (about 15-20 minutes).

Cornish treacle tart

For flaky pastry
6 oz plain flour
pinch of salt
2 oz butter
2 oz lard
3-4 fl oz ice-cold water

For filling
8 tablespoons white bread crumbs
1 teacup golden syrup
grated rind and juice of $\frac{1}{2}$ lemon
caster sugar (for dusting)

6-7 inch diameter sandwich tin, or pie plate

Method
Make the flaky pastry: sift flour and salt into a bowl. Divide fats into four portions (two butter, two lard); rub one portion into the flour and mix to a firm dough with cold water. Knead dough lightly until smooth, then roll out to an oblong. Put a second portion of fat (not the same kind as portion rubbed in) in small pieces on to two-thirds of dough. Fold in three, turn dough to bring the open edge towards you and roll out again to an oblong. Put on a third portion of fat in pieces, fold dough in three, wrap in a cloth and leave in a cool place for 15 minutes. Roll out again, put on remaining fat in pieces, fold and roll to an oblong 12 inches by 7 inches.

Set oven at 425°F or Mark 7.

Mix the breadcrumbs, syrup, and lemon flavouring together. Cut pastry into two. Roll one piece a little thinner, line on to tin or pie plate and damp the edges.

Spread filling over the pastry lining the tin and cover with remaining pastry. Seal pastry edges, brush top with water and sprinkle with sugar. Bake for 30-40 minutes.

Bakewell tart

6 oz rich shortcrust pastry

For filling
1 tablespoon strawberry jam
1 tablespoon lemon curd (page 23)
1 oz butter
2 oz caster sugar
grated rind and juice of $\frac{1}{2}$ lemon
1 egg
2 oz ground almonds
2 rounded tablespoons cake crumbs

7-inch diameter sandwich tin

Method
Make the pastry and set aside to chill (see method, page 12). When chilled, roll it out and line on to the sandwich tin, knock up and scallop pastry edges. Spread the pastry first with jam and then with lemon curd.

Cream the butter in a bowl until soft, add the sugar and lemon rind and continue beating until light. Beat egg, add a little at a time, and then stir in the almonds, cake crumbs and lemon juice. Spread the almond mixture over the lemon curd and bake for 35-45 minutes until set and golden-brown in an oven at 375°F or Mark 5.

Tarte aux pruneaux (Prune flan)

¾ lb prunes
¼ pint red wine (Burgundy, or
   Claret)
3 tablespoons redcurrant jelly

For almond pastry
6 oz flour
4 oz butter
1½ oz ground almonds
1½ oz caster sugar
1 egg yolk
1-2 tablespoons cold water

For custard cream
1 rounded tablespoon custard
   powder
¼ pint milk
¼ pint double cream (whipped)
1 teaspoon caster sugar

For almond filling
2 oz ground almonds
1½ tablespoons caster sugar
½ egg white (beaten)

7-8 inch diameter flan ring

Method

Soak prunes in wine for 2-3 hours. Prepare pastry as for shortcrust (see method, page 21), adding almonds and sugar after rubbing in fat and before mixing with egg yolk and water. Chill pastry in refrigerator for 30 minutes. Roll out and line into flan ring ; bake blind.

Simmer the prunes in the wine until tender.

Watchpoint Prunes must be cooked very gently and in a pan with a tight-fitting lid because there is so little liquid.

Lift prunes from pan with a draining spoon and set aside to cool. Add redcurrant jelly to pan and set on a low heat to melt. Whisk, if necessary, to get glaze smooth, then strain.

Put custard powder in a small pan, mix to a smooth paste with milk and stir over a gentle heat until boiling ; tip into a basin and whisk well. When quite cold, whip cream, sweeten with sugar, fold into custard.

Cut prunes carefully down one side and remove stones.

To prepare almond filling : combine all filling ingredients, adding just enough egg white to bind mixture together and fill this into the prunes.

Spoon the custard cream into flan case, spreading it evenly. Arrange filled prunes over top to cover cream. Brush or spoon glaze over the flan.

1 *Remove stones, fill prunes neatly with the almond mixture*
2 *Pour custard cream into the flan case, spreading it evenly*
3 *Arrange prunes on top to cover the cream completely*
4 *Spoon on cooled redcurrant glaze and then leave it to set*

Lemon chiffon pie

American crumb shell (see right),
or 6-8 oz quantity rich shortcrust pastry (see method, page 17)

For filling
2 eggs (separated)
4 oz caster sugar
pinch of salt
juice of 1 small lemon and
grated rind of ½ lemon
1 teaspoon powdered gelatine
(soaked in 1 tablespoon cold
water)
pinch of cream of tartar
1 small carton (2½ fl oz double
cream

*8-inch diameter pie plate, or 8-inch
diameter flan ring (buttered)*

*Lemon chiffon pie: crumb case
with a light creamy filling*

Method
Fill the pie plate, or line flan
ring with American crumb shell,
or shortcrust pastry, and bake
blind.

Beat egg yolks with 2 oz
sugar, salt, lemon juice and
rind; pour all into a double
saucepan, cook and stir until
thick. Remove the pan from the
heat, add the soaked gelatine,
stir in well and leave to cool.

Whisk the egg whites with
the cream of tartar until foaming,
then add the remaining sugar
a dessertspoon at a time, and
continue whisking until stiff
and glossy. Whisk the cream
until thick.

When the lemon mixture
begins to set, beat with a rotary
whisk until smooth and then
fold it into the meringue with
the cream.

Pile the mixture into the
cooled pie shell or flan and
chill until set. Take out of the
refrigerator 20 minutes before
serving.

American crumb shell

5 oz biscuit crumbs
4 oz caster sugar
4 oz butter (melted)

8-inch diameter pie plate 2-2½ inches deep, or 8-inch diameter flan ring

This pie crust is very popular and is used with fresh fruit and cream or chiffon pies. Make with an unsweetened biscuit — a Cornish wafer is very suitable.

Method
Crush the biscuits with a rolling pin and rub them through a wire sieve or strainer into a mixing bowl. Add the sugar and melted butter. Press the mixture thickly over bottom and sides of buttered pie plate or flan ring.

Chill pie crust before filling or, alternatively, bake blind in oven pre-set at 375°F or Mark 5, for 10 minutes and then chill.

American crumb shell is pressed down to coat flan ring thickly

Butterscotch cream pie

6-8 oz rich shortcrust pastry
(see method, page 17)

For filling
2 oz butter
4 oz dark brown sugar
¼ pint boiling water
2 tablespoons cornflour
1 tablespoon flour
large pinch of salt
½ pint milk
2 egg yolks (beaten)
2 drops of vanilla essence

To decorate
¼ pint double cream (whipped)
2 tablespoons almonds (browned and finely chopped)

8-inch diameter flan ring

Method
Line the flan ring with the pastry, bake blind and chill cooked flan case.

Melt the butter in a heavy frying pan or saucepan and when golden-brown add the brown sugar; stir until foaming and boil for 2-3 minutes. Remove from the heat and stir in the boiling water.

Place the cornflour, flour and salt in a saucepan and mix to a smooth paste with the milk, then add the brown sugar mixture. Stir over gentle heat until boiling and then cook for 1 minute.

Pour half the mixture on to the beaten egg yolks, return this to remainder in the pan and continue cooking for 1 minute; add vanilla essence. Pour the mixture into the baked pastry flan and chill again.

Cover the top with the whipped cream and decorate with the almonds.

Almond and apricot flan

1 lb fresh apricots
sugar syrup (made by dissolving 3
    tablespoons granulated sugar in
    ½ pint water)
2 tablespoons apricot jam (sieved)
1 rounded teaspoon arrowroot
    (mixed with 1 tablespoon
    water) — optional
¼-½ pint double cream (whipped,
    seetened with little caster sugar
    and flavoured with kirsch)
few almonds (blanched and split)
    — see page 13

For almond pastry
1 oz shortening
3 oz butter
6 oz plain flour
1½ oz ground almonds
1½ oz caster sugar
1 egg yolk
1-2 tablespoons cold water

8-inch diameter flan ring

Method
Prepare sugar syrup for poaching the fruit. Halve and stone apricots, and place them, rounded side down, in a pan with syrup and bring very slowly to boil. Allow syrup to boil up and over fruit and then reduce heat, cover pan and leave to simmer very gently until tender.

Even fully ripe fruit must be thoroughly cooked to allow the syrup to penetrate, sweeten and prevent discolouration.

Prepare the pastry. Rub the fats into the flour, add the ground almonds and sugar. Mix the egg yolk with water and add to the dry ingredients. Work lightly to a firm dough and chill slightly. Roll out, line into flan ring and bake blind for about 10-15 minutes at 375°F or Mark 5. After 10 minutes, when pastry is firm, remove paper and beans (used for baking blind) and continue cooking for 3-5 minutes to dry bottom of flan. Pastry should not colour.

Drain the apricots, boil the juice until thick and syrupy, then add jam and stir until melted. Strain and if glaze is too runny, thicken with the slaked arrowroot; allow this glaze to cool before using.

When flan case is quite cold, fill with whipped cream, arrange the apricots and almonds on top and brush with glaze.

Take up the apricot halves and carefully arrange them to cover the flan

The finished flan decorated with the blanched almonds and apricot glaze

Fruit crust pies with apple or peach filling

For American pastry
7 oz lard, or commercially prepared shortening, eg. Spry, Cookeen
4 tablespoons water
11 oz plain flour
$\frac{1}{4}$ teaspoon salt

For apple filling
2 lb Pippin apples (peeled and cored)
$\frac{1}{2}$ teaspoon freshly ground cinnamon
grated rind and juice of 1 lemon
little butter

For peach filling
1 large can sliced peaches
4 fresh peaches
little butter

Two 7-8 inch diameter pie plates

This quantity of pastry will make 2 pies.

Method

To make the American pastry, put the lard (or shortening) and water into a mixing bowl and work together with a wooden spoon until creamy. Sift the flour with the salt into the bowl and cut and stir with a round-bladed knife until all the ingredients are well blended. Gather the dough together with the fingertips, press it firmly into a ball, wrap it in waxed paper and chill before using.

Divide the pastry in four, and roll out two pieces into rounds about $\frac{1}{8}$ inch thick and 1 inch larger than the pie plates to allow for depth. Keep the pastry round as it is being rolled and be careful not to add extra flour as this will make it too tough. Fold the rounds in half, or lift them one at a time on the rolling pin, and quickly line them into the pie plates. Avoid stretching the pastry, and trim the edges with a knife or scissors.

Set the oven at 425°F or Mark 7. Slice the apples, and fill one of the pies, doming the fruit, and add the cinnamon and lemon juice.

For the other pie, drain the canned peaches well; scald, peel and slice the fresh peaches and mix them with the canned ones. Fill into the pie.

Dot both fruits with butter, and moisten the edges of the pastry with water.

Roll out the remaining pieces of pastry a little thinner than the bottom crusts and 1 inch larger than the plates. Fold in half. Make several slits near the centres, and lift them carefully on to the pies. Unfold the pastry and fold the overhanging pastry under the lower layer. Seal the edges and flute with your forefinger and thumb.

Bake in the pre-set hot oven for 15 minutes, then reduce the heat to 400°F or Mark 6, and bake for a further 20-30 minutes. Serve warm.

Puddings

Hot steamed, boiled and baked puddings are an essential part of the English diet. Spicy or sweet, rich or plain, they form an ideal insulation against our damp, chilly winters.

In the old days they supplemented an inadequate meat diet for the poor, and spread the repast of the wealthy to sumptuous proportions. Today they remain favourites for family meals and in their richest forms continue to grace our tables on the most festive occasions — Christmas pudding being the prime example.

Diet-conscious cooks may prefer to avoid the heavier puddings in their everyday fare, but as a treat for the family or when entertaining, they are a guaranteed 'recipe for success'.

Steamed and boiled puddings are particularly English. In steaming, the food does not come into contact with the boiling water but only with its vapour. This is usually done in a steamer — a container with perforations at the bottom and a close fitting lid. This can be bought with graduated ridges at the base rim so that it will fit snugly on to saucepans of varying sizes. Alternatively, the basin can be placed directly in a saucepan, with boiling water to come not more than half way up the basin.

A pudding can also be boiled, covering the basin with water completely and cooking for a rather shorter time.

A suet pudding should be rich yet light. To get this result, breadcrumbs can be used to lighten the flour, and butcher's suet for flavour.

Some steamed and baked puddings, a little lighter in texture than a suet pudding, are made by the same method as plain cake mixtures. Here the fat is rubbed into the flour. Butter is used to give the best flavour, but this can be replaced by margarine or a commercially prepared shortening.

Lighter still are the steamed sponge puddings made just like rich, creamed cake mixtures. These make wonderful nursery puddings.

The following recipe gives the basic proportions for a suet pudding. At any time, up to half the flour can be replaced with the same weight of fresh bread-crumbs.

Basic recipe

8 oz plain flour

3-5 oz butcher's suet

$\frac{1}{2}$ teaspoon salt

2 teaspoons baking powder, or $\frac{1}{2}$ teaspoon bicarbonate of soda if treacle is used in recipe and you like a dark pudding

1-4 oz sugar

1-4 tablespoons treacle, golden syrup, marmalade or jam, or 2-6 oz dried fruit

1 egg

milk (about $\frac{1}{4}$ pint if no other liquid is used)

Method

Well grease a pudding basin and have ready a saucepan of boiling water. (If boiling the pudding, there should be enough water to cover the basin completely; if steaming without a steamer, the water should not come more than half-way up the basin.)

Sieve the flour with the salt and baking powder (or bicarbonate of soda) into a mixing bowl. If using fresh butcher's suet, remove skin, shred and chop finely, removing membranes.(Use a little of the measured flour to prevent suet sticking). Add the remaining ingredients to the flour, using enough milk to give a dropping consistency (ie. so that it just drops from a wooden spoon when shaken).

Mix well and turn at once into the prepared basin. Cover with pieces of well-buttered grease-proof paper and foil, both with two 1-inch pleats in the centre, at right-angles to each other, to allow the pudding to rise. Tie down with string. For boiling, cover with a scalded cloth, floured on the underside and pleated in the centre; tie the cloth round the basin rim with string, and knot the four corners back over the top. Make a loop of string after tying to prevent burnt hands when removing the basin from the steamer.

Boil for $2\frac{1}{2}$ hours, or steam for 3 hours, ensuring that the water is kept boiling all the time and topped up regularly with boiling water.

Date pudding

4 oz self-raising flour
½ teaspoon mixed spice
pinch of salt
3 oz butter
4 rounded tablespoons fresh
  breadcrumbs (see page 154)
2 rounded tablespoons soft brown
  sugar
4 oz dates (stoned and chopped)
2 eggs
1 tablespoon golden syrup
1-2 tablespoons milk

Method
Sift flour with spice and salt
into a bowl. Rub in butter and
stir in breadcrumbs, sugar and
chopped dates. Whisk eggs
with syrup and milk, tip into the
dry ingredients and mix with a
wooden spoon until smooth,
adding extra milk, if necessary.

Turn into a well-greased
basin, cover with greaseproof
paper and foil, pleated across
the centre, tie securely and
steam for 1½-2 hours. Serve with
custard or custard sauce (see
page 101).

Eve's pudding

3 large cooking apples
2 tablespoons granulated sugar
grated rind and juice of ½ lemon
1 tablespoon water
3 oz butter
3 oz caster sugar
1 large egg
5 oz self-raising flour
pinch of salt
2-3 tablespoons milk
custard, or cream (optional)

6-inch diameter pie dish

Method
Peel and core the apples, cut in
thick slices and put in a pan
with granulated sugar, lemon
juice and water; cook until apple
is tender. Place at the bottom of
a pie dish.

Soften the butter with the
lemon rind in a bowl, add the
caster sugar and work until light
and fluffy. Beat in the egg and
then with a metal spoon fold in
the flour sifted with the salt
(this is to avoid losing any of
the air beaten into the egg).
Stir in enough milk to give a
mixture of dropping consistency.

Spread the mixture over the
apple and bake for about 40
minutes in an oven at 375°F or
Mark 5. Serve hot with custard
or cream, if wished.

Apple hat

8 oz self-raising flour
pinch of salt
4-5 oz suet
6-8 tablespoons cold water (to mix)
1-1½ lb cooking apples
2 tablespoons demerara sugar
grated rind ½ lemon, or 2-3 cloves
4-5 tablespoons water

6-inch diameter pudding basin

Method

Sift flour with salt into a mixing bowl. If using fresh butcher's suet, remove skin, shred and chop finely using a little of the measured flour to prevent it sticking. Mix suet with flour and work quickly to a light dough with cold water. Knead lightly. Well grease basin and have ready a steamer or saucepan of boiling water.

Roll out pastry to a round 6-7 inches in diameter, dust centre with flour and fold in half. Make a large dart in double layer of pastry, tapering to a point on the fold. Then roll out folded end, from point of dart, thus forming a 'pocket' that will fit the bottom of the pudding basin (see photographs, right).

Lift pastry carefully and line it into the basin (some of the pastry will overhang the sides); brush away any surplus flour.

Peel, core and slice apples into basin, layering them with the sugar and lemon rind or cloves; spoon over water. Damp pastry edges, draw this thicker, overhanging section up and over fruit and press firmly together. For steaming cover with a piece of well buttered greaseproof paper and foil; for boiling cover with a scalded cloth. Boil for 2-2½ hours, or steam for 2½-3 hours. Then take up pudding, remove cloth or foil and greaseproof and leave for 3-4 minutes before turning out on to a plate. Serve hot with custard or cream and brown sugar.

1 *After folding pastry in half, make a large dart in double layer of pastry from open edges, tapering to a point on the fold. Roll out the folded end from point of dart, forming a pocket*
2 *Place your fist carefully inside pocket and lift pastry, lining it into the basin (some pastry will overhang the sides). Layer apples into the basin, dampen pastry edges and draw up overhanging pastry over fruit. Press edges together*
3 and 4 *Butter a piece of greaseproof paper, and make two 1-inch pleats in centre, at right angles to each other, to allow pudding to rise. Cover basin, and tie down securely with string. Repeat process with foil*

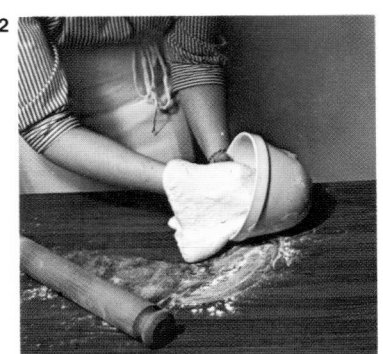

Christmas pudding

8 oz self-raising flour
1 teaspoon salt
½ nutmeg (grated)
1 teaspoon mixed spice
12 oz fresh white breadcrumbs
12 oz beef suet
4 oz demerara sugar
1 lb currants
1 lb sultanas
2 lb raisins (stoned)
4 oz candied peel
2 tablespoons almonds (blanched
   and shredded) — see page 13
1 large cooking apple (peeled and
   grated)
rind and juice of 1 orange
6 eggs
¼ pint milk, or ale, or stout

*4 medium-size pudding basins, or
1 large and 2 small ones*

Method

Well grease basins; have ready a fish kettle or sufficient large saucepans of boiling water.

Sift flour with salt and spices into a very large mixing bowl, add all dry ingredients and grated apple and mix well together. Beat eggs until frothy, add orange juice and milk, ale, or stout; add to mixture. Stir well. Turn into prepared basins, fill them to the top with mixture.

Butter a large round of greaseproof paper for each basin, cut a piece of foil to same size. Put both rounds together, foil uppermost, fold across centre to form a 1-inch pleat and lay over basins with buttered, greaseproof side next to pudding mixture. Tie down securely with string, leaving a loop for easy removal when cooked. Place basins in fish kettle, or saucepans, with enough fast boiling water to cover. Cook large puddings for 6 hours, small ones for 4 hours. Boil steadily, replenishing with boiling water from time to time.

When cooked, lift basins out carefully, leave foil and greaseproof paper on puddings until cold before retying with freshly-buttered greaseproof paper and foil and storing in dry cupboard.
Watchpoint It's important that puddings do not go off the boil.

When ready to serve at Christmas, boil or steam a further 2 hours. Brandy or rum butter should be served separately (see page 149).

Toffee pudding

6 slices of light milk bread, or
  Sally Lunn tea cake
$\frac{1}{3}$ pint sugar syrup — see below, or
  1 teacup milk mixed with 1 beaten
  egg

For toffee mixture
3 oz butter
4 rounded tablespoons sugar
6 tablespoons golden syrup
1-2 cartons plain yoghourt
sugar (to sweeten)

Sugar syrup
To make $\frac{1}{2}$ pint sugar syrup :
Heat 8 oz sugar and $\frac{1}{4}$ pint water
gently in a pan until sugar is
dissolved. Then bring to boil and
boil steadily for 10 minutes
(220°F on a sugar thermometer).

Method
Cut the bread (or tea cake)
evenly into 1-inch thick slices,
removing crusts, then cut each
slice in two. Moisten them with
a little sugar syrup (or dip into
the milk and egg).

To prepare toffee mixture,
put half the butter, half the
sugar and half the golden
syrup into a frying pan, cook
until it is turning colour, then
at once put in the bread (or tea
cake) pieces and continue to
cook until brown on one side,
then turn and brown on the
other.

Place pieces in a circle in a
buttered dish, overlapping the
slices and leaving a space in the
centre.

Wipe out the pan and cook
a little more toffee mixture,
using the remaining ingredients.
Spoon or pour this over the
pieces in the dish. Fill the centre
with the yoghourt, lightly
sweetened, and serve at once.

Belvoir pudding

2 oz mixed glacé cherries and
   angelica
4 oz self-raising flour
pinch of salt
1 tablespoon instant coffee
2 tablespoons water
4 oz butter
4 oz caster sugar
2 eggs (lightly beaten)

*Fluted, or plain, cake tin, or ring
   mould, or loaf tin (1 pint capacity)*

We like to cook this pudding in
a fluted cake tin but it can also
be prepared in one of the other
tins suggested.

Method
Butter and flour the tin and set
the oven at 350°F or Mark 4.

If the cherries are very sticky,
quickly wash them in hot water,
then drain and dry them well.
Chop both the cherries and
angelica, mix together and dust
with a tablespoon of the measured flour. Sift the remaining
flour with a pinch of salt and
dissolve the coffee in the water.

Soften the butter in a bowl,
add the sugar and work together
until mixture is light and fluffy.
Beat in the eggs, a little at a
time, then use a metal spoon to
fold in the flour, coffee and
fruit. Turn mixture into the prepared tin and bake for about 40
minutes. The pudding is ready
when risen and spongy to the
touch and when a warm skewer
or knife inserted comes out
clean.

Serve pudding on a hot dish,
dusted with caster sugar, and
hand a mousseline sauce (see
page 145) or rum butter (see
149) separately.

Gingerbread pudding

½ lb packet of ginger nuts
¼ pint double cream
1 teaspoon caster sugar
1 small can (11 oz) mandarin
   oranges (drained)

This pudding should be made
the day before it is to be eaten.

Method
Lightly whip the cream, then
sweeten a little with the sugar.
Take a small round casserole
and put on the bottom a layer
of broken ginger nuts. Cover
this with a layer of mandarin
oranges and cover this in turn
with a thin layer of whipped
cream.

Repeat this layering until all
the ingredients have been used,
finishing with cream. Cover
casserole with lid or foil and
leave in refrigerator overnight.

Upside-down gingerbread

4 oz flour
½ teaspoon bicarbonate of soda
¼ teaspoon salt
2 teaspoons cinnamon
1 teaspoon ground ginger
¼ teaspoon grated nutmeg
pinch of ground cloves
1 egg (beaten)
4 oz soft brown sugar
3 oz black treacle
4 fl oz sour milk
2 oz shortening (melted)

For topping
2 oz butter
3-4 oz soft brown sugar
1 medium-size can pears (drained
   from their syrup)
few walnuts
whipped cream, or cream cheese
   and top of milk, or soured cream
   sauce (optional)

8-inch diameter, or square, cake tin

*Arrange pears and walnuts in tin
and cover with gingerbread mixture*

Method

First make the topping. Melt the butter, add the brown sugar and stir for 1-2 minutes over gentle heat and then pour into tin. Arrange the pears around the tin with the walnuts positioned in between.

Set the oven at 350-375°F or Mark 4-5.

To make the gingerbread: mix and sift the flour, bicarbonate of soda, salt and spices. Mix together egg, sugar, black treacle, sour milk and cooled shortening. Stir into the flour mixture, beat hard for 1 minute or until smooth, and pour on top of the fruit.

Bake the gingerbread in preset oven for 40-50 minutes.

Turn out on to a serving plate. Serve warm, with whipped cream, or with cream cheese thinned with the top of the milk until the consistency of whipped cream, or with soured cream sauce.

Soured cream sauce

Whip one small carton of double cream until it just holds its shape, then stir in one carton of plain yoghourt.

When turned out, gingerbread is patterned with pears and walnuts ; serve with soured cream sauce

Rich fig pudding

8 oz dried figs
4 oz raisins (stoned)
8 oz dates (stoned)
3 oz stem ginger
2-3 tablespoons brandy, or rum
6 oz fresh white breadcrumbs
8 oz self-raising flour
6 oz shredded suet
good pinch of salt
3 eggs
grated rind and juice of 1 lemon
a little milk (optional)
maple syrup (optional)

Pudding basin (2 pints capacity)

Method

Slice the fruit and ginger, mix together and sprinkle with the brandy or rum. Cover and leave for 1 hour or longer. Mix well together the crumbs, flour, suet and salt. Beat the eggs to a froth and mix into the dry ingredients with the lemon rind and juice, and the fruit. Mix thoroughly, adding a little milk if necessary to bring the mixture to a dropping consistency.

Turn into well-greased basin, cover, and steam for 4 hours. Turn out, pour round a little maple syrup (bought), or serve with a hard sauce (see page 149).

Slicing the fruit and ginger before sprinkling with brandy

Adding the brandy-flavoured fruit to the suet mixture

This rich fig pudding can be served with maple syrup or hard sauce

Chocolate puddings

3 oz plain chocolate
¼ pint milk
5 oz stale cake crumbs
2 oz butter
2 rounded tablespoons caster sugar
2 large eggs (separated)
2-3 drops of vanilla essence

8 castle pudding tins (small moulds)

Method

Cut up the chocolate, melt it slowly in the milk in a saucepan, then bring to the boil and pour over the cake crumbs in a basin. Mix well with a fork, cover and leave to stand for 20-30 minutes.

Have ready a steamer over a pan of boiling water.

Soften the butter in a bowl, add the sugar and work until mixture is light. Beat in the egg yolks and then add the soaked crumbs and vanilla. Whisk the egg whites until stiff and use a metal spoon to fold them carefully into the mixture.

Divide mixture into the buttered pudding tins, cover with foil, or with a piece of buttered greaseproof paper, tie down securely and steam until set (45-50 minutes). Turn on to a hot dish, dust with caster sugar and serve with whipped cream or hot chocolate sauce (see page 146).

Chocolate puddings served with a hot chocolate sauce

Spotted dick

8 oz self-raising flour
pinch of salt
4 oz butter
2 rounded tablespoons caster sugar
6 oz currants (washed)
2 eggs
little milk

Method
Sift the flour with the salt into a basin, rub in butter and then stir in the sugar and currants. Whisk the eggs, add to the mixture and stir until smooth with a wooden spoon, adding milk, if necessary, to give a dropping consistency.

Turn into a well-greased basin, cover as before, tie securely and steam for $1\frac{1}{2}$-2 hours. Serve with custard or syrup sauce.

Spotted dick with a syrup sauce

Steamed ginger pudding

10 oz flour
1 rounded teaspoon ground ginger
good pinch of mixed spice
1 teaspoon bicarbonate of soda
5 oz shredded suet
1 large egg (beaten)
6 fl oz (6 tablespoons) golden syrup, or treacle
approximately 6 fl oz milk

6-7 inch diameter pudding basin

Method
Sift the flour, spices and bi-carbonate of soda into a bowl. Add the suet, mix and make a well in the centre. Pour in the egg and syrup (or treacle). Warm the milk until tepid and pour into the bowl. Stir well: the mixture should drop easily from the spoon.

Have the pudding basin well greased, turn mixture into it and cover with a pleated piece of oiled or greaseproof paper. Stand basin in a large pan of boiling water, which should come between half and two-thirds of the way up the sides of the basin. Cover pan and steam for about $2\frac{1}{2}$-3 hours, remembering to fill the pan with extra boiling water if necessary.

Turn out to serve, accompanied by warm golden syrup or custard sauce.

Valencia pudding

6 oz raisins (stoned)
6 oz butter
grated rind and juice of $\frac{1}{2}$ lemon
6 oz caster sugar
3 eggs
6 oz self-raising flour
pinch of salt

Charlotte tin (1$\frac{1}{2}$ pints capacity), or 5-inch diameter pudding basin

Method
Well grease the charlotte tin or basin and have ready a steamer over a pan of boiling water.

Split and press enough raisins (skin side against the prepared tin or basin) to cover the bottom and to make a pattern up the sides. Cut the remaining raisins into small pieces. Soften the butter with the lemon rind in a bowl, add the sugar and beat well until mixture is light and fluffy.

Beat in the eggs one at a time with 1 teaspoon flour. Sift the remaining flour with salt and use a metal spoon to fold into the mixture with the lemon juice and remaining raisins. Spoon carefully into prepared tin or basin. Cover with buttered greaseproof paper and foil (with a 1-inch pleat to allow pudding to rise) and steam for 2 hours. Serve with custard (see page 101) or a mousseline sauce (see page 145).

Six-cup pudding

1 teacup plain flour
pinch of salt
1 teacup fresh breadcrumbs
1 teacup caster sugar
1 teacup suet (chopped)
1 teacup milk
$\frac{1}{2}$ teaspoon bicarbonate of soda
1 teacup strawberry jam

Method
Mix sifted flour with the salt in a bowl and mix with the bread-crumbs, sugar and suet; warm the milk very slightly in a saucepan, add the bicarbonate of soda and stir into dry ingredients with the jam. Turn at once into, and threequarters fill, a well-greased basin. Cover with pleated, buttered grease-proof paper and foil, tie securely and steam for 3 hours. Serve with lemon butter (see page 147), or custard sauce (see page 101).

Meringues

Meringues are not difficult to make and are ideal for party meals, prepared well in advance and served with fruit and cream. The texture is creamy, and the mixture can be formed into the most decorative shapes.

Meringue is a mixture of egg white and sugar. It is thought to have been invented in the early 18th century by Gasparini, a Swiss pastrycook, in the town of Mehrinyghen — hence 'meringue'.

There are three distinct types of meringue used for various sweet course dishes, gâteaux and pâtisseries: suisse, cuite and italienne.

1 Meringue suisse is the one most frequently made. The proportion of sugar to egg white never varies, being 2 oz caster sugar to each egg white, which is stiffly whipped before the sugar is folded in. The number of egg whites varies according to the recipe.

This meringue is used in sweets such as vacherin (large rounds of meringue filled with whipped cream, fruit, chestnuts etc.) or as a topping for pies. The most simple way to use

this type is in meringue shells filled with whipped cream (see recipe for Meringue Chantilly on pages 52-53).

2 Meringue cuite (cooked) is a slight misnomer as it is not actually cooked in the making. It is firmer than meringue suisse and used mainly for meringue baskets and pâtisseries.

Proportions are 2 oz icing sugar to each egg white (you can be generous with the weight of sugar) and it can be made in large quantities with an electric whisk. If whisking by hand it is quicker to put the bowl of egg whites over a pan of hot water, as the heat quickens up the thickening process.

3 Meringue italienne is really more for professionals and those engaged in pâtisserie work. It is similar to meringue cuite but a lighter and finer mixture. It takes some skill to make as the lump sugar is made into a syrup and boiled to a certain degree before being poured on to the egg whites. It is essential to use a sugar thermometer for this meringue.

Though the sugar for meringues can be measured by the tablespoon, it is wiser to use scales to ensure a uniform result.

For meringue shells or a vacherin-type sweet, a special copper bowl and a balloon whisk are best, but not essential. The shape of the bowl and slightly rounded whisk make for greater bulk of egg whites. There is also less risk of overbeating, which so often happens when an electric mixer or rotary whisk is employed. If you don't have a copper bowl, whisk whites to a froth only with a rotary whisk or mixer, then whisk by hand with a balloon whisk until a firm snow.

For meringue cuite and meringue italienne, use a rotary whisk in a pudding basin, rather than a mixing bowl (which is larger and more suitable for mixing or beating), or use an electric mixer.

Chamonix

For meringue
2 egg whites
4 oz caster sugar

For chestnut purée
1 lb chestnuts
1 vanilla pod
2 tablespoons sugar
4 tablespoons water

For cream filling
$\frac{1}{4}$ pint double cream
1 teaspoon caster sugar
2 drops of vanilla essence
1 egg white
1 tablespoon chocolate (grated)

Method

Line a baking sheet with non-stick (silicone) cooking paper. Set oven at 275°F or Mark $\frac{1}{2}$-1.

To prepare the meringue: whisk egg whites until stiff, add 1 tablespoon of the sugar and continue whisking for about 1 minute. Fold in remaining sugar with a metal spoon. Spread or pipe into a circle 9 inches in diameter. Bake until crisp, dry and pale biscuit-coloured (for about 1 hour). Skin chestnuts, cook with the vanilla pod for flavour, drain (reserving liquid) and sieve. Dissolve sugar in water, boil and cool in a small bowl. Work cooled syrup into chestnut purée and add 1-2 tablespoons of the cooking liquid to make the mixture easy to pipe. Put into a forcing bag, using a very small plain nozzle.

Turn the cream into a cold basin, whisk until thick, then add the sugar and essence. Whip the egg white until stiff, add to the cream and whisk together until it holds shape.

When the meringue is quite cold, pipe the chestnut to form a nest. Fill the centre with cream and dust with chocolate.

To skin and cook chestnuts :
Put them into a pan and cover with plenty of cold water. Bring to the boil and, once the water is bubbling well, remove the pan from the heat. Take nuts out of water (use a draining spoon); hold with a cloth while stripping off the peel and inner skin with a small, sharp knife. If skin doesn't come away easily, put the nut back into the pan for a further minute. If the water cools, bring it up again to the boil. Don't let the water. Cook them gently until tender (about 20-30 minutes). minute, or nuts will cook and peel and skin be impossible to remove.

Once skinned, put the nuts into a pan, and cover with a mixture of half milk, half water. Cook them gently until tender (about 20-30 minutes). Then drain and sieve, or use according to recipe. Once cooked and sieved, they can be stored in a deep freeze.

If you are using dried chestnuts, take half the quantity in recipe and soak in cold water overnight. Drain, then cover with milk and water and cook about 20 minutes until tender.

Meringue Chantilly

For meringue suisse
4 egg whites
8 oz caster sugar (plus extra for dredging)
$\frac{1}{2}$ pint Chantilly cream
salad oil (for baking sheets)
flour (for dredging)

These are meringue shells filled with vanilla-flavoured whipped cream. This quantity will make 12-16 shells (6-8 filled meringues). Unfilled shells may be stored for up to 2 days in an airtight container.

Method

Set oven at 250-275°F or Mark $\frac{1}{2}$-1. Brush 2 baking sheets lightly with oil and dredge with flour. Bang sheets on the table to distribute the flour evenly, or line the sheets with non-stick (silicone) cooking paper.

Whisk the egg whites until quite stiff; they should look smooth and when a little is lifted on the whisk it should remain in position when shaken. For each egg white whisk in 1 teaspoon of sugar for 1 minute only. Fold in remaining sugar with a metal spoon.

Put meringue into a forcing bag with a plain nozzle and pipe shells on to prepared baking sheets (or put out in spoonfuls). Dredge with caster sugar and leave for a few minutes before putting into oven to allow the

Taking up meringue mixture with two spoons to form shell shape

Laying shells on to baking sheet before dredging with caster sugar

sugar to melt slightly, giving a crystallised effect to the meringues when cooked.

Bake for about 1 hour, changing round the trays halfway through (top shelf being warmer than second shelf). When meringues are set, carefully lift them from the sheet with a sharp knife, or peel off the non-stick paper.

Gently press underneath to form a hollow, put back on the sheets on their sides, and replace in the oven to allow the undersides to dry for 20-30 minutes. Lift on to a rack to cool.

The shells are hollowed so that they can hold a fair proportion of cream and the two halves will not slip when sandwiched together.

A meringue of this type should be delicate beige in colour, crisp in texture and slightly sticky.

Serve within 1-2 hours of filling with Chantilly cream.

Chantilly cream

Turn $\frac{1}{2}$ pint of double cream into a cold basin and, using a fork or open wire whisk, whisk gently until it thickens. Add 3-4 teaspoons caster sugar to taste and 2-3 drops of vanilla essence and continue whisking until the cream will hold its shape.

For a delicate flavour, instead of the essence, sweeten with vanilla sugar (made by storing 1-2 vanilla pods in a jar of sugar), and a few of the seeds scraped from a vanilla pod.

Alternatively, piping out shells with plain nozzle before baking

Apple meringue or Apple amber

3 large cooking apples (about 1½ lb)
3 tablespoons granulated sugar
rind and juice of ½ lemon
1 oz butter
2 egg yolks

For meringue
2 egg whites
small pinch of salt
4 oz caster sugar

6-inch diameter pie dish

Method
Cook apples to purée as follows: thinly peel, quarter and core apples, slice into a saucepan, add sugar and grated rind and juice of ½ lemon. Cover with buttered paper and lid and cook gently to a pulp, stirring occasionally. Crush with a potato masher or beat well with a wooden spoon.

Beat in butter a small piece at a time while purée is hot and follow with the yolks. Pour mixture into a pie dish.

Whisk egg whites with salt until stiff in a bowl, add 2 teaspoons of the measured sugar and beat for half a minute. Fold in remaining sugar with a metal spoon and then pile on top of apple. Dust with caster sugar and bake for about 30 minutes until top is crisp and golden-brown in the oven at 325°F or Mark 3.

Chocolate meringue pie

6-8 oz quantity rich shortcrust pastry (see method, page 17)

For filling
2 oz cocoa
4 oz granulated sugar
pinch of salt
2 tablespoons cornflour
1 dessertspoon flour
1 pint milk
2 egg yolks (beaten)
1 oz butter
3-4 drops of vanilla essence

For meringue
2 egg whites
pinch of cream of tartar
4 oz caster sugar

8-inch diameter flan ring

Method
Line the flan ring with the pastry and bake blind.

Put the cocoa, sugar, salt, cornflour and flour in a saucepan and mix them to a smooth paste with the milk. Stir over gentle heat until boiling and cook for 1 minute. Pour half the mixture on to the beaten egg yolks, return this to remainder in the pan and cook for 1 minute. Beat in the butter and vanilla essence and pour mixture into prepared pastry flan.

Now prepare the meringue: whisk the egg whites with the cream of tartar until foaming, add the sugar gradually and continue whisking until stiff and glossy. Pile this on to the chocolate filling, being careful to seal the meringue on to the pastry and so prevent shrinking. Bake in the oven at 350°F or Mark 4 for 8-10 minutes or till lightly browned. Serve cold.

Coffee and walnut galette

4 egg whites
8 oz caster sugar
24 walnut kernels
extra caster, or icing, sugar (for dusting)
¾ pint double cream

For filling
1 pint strong black coffee
3 tablespoons custard powder
sugar (to taste)

2 baking sheets lined with non-stick (silicone) kitchen paper; forcing bag and ½ inch plain nozzle

Method
Set oven at 290°F or Mark 1.

Whip egg whites until stiff but not dry, add 1 tablespoon of the sugar and continue whisking for about 30 seconds; then, using a metal spoon, cut and fold in the remaining sugar. Put mixture in the forcing bag and pipe out an 8-inch round on one baking sheet; dust lightly with sugar and let it stand while shaping rest of mixture into very small rounds on the second baking sheet.

Place a walnut half on top of each meringue and dust with a little sugar. Put the plain round on a shelf about halfway in the oven and the small meringues on the shelf underneath. Bake until crisp and biscuit-coloured (about 1 hour). Cool meringues on a wire rack.

To prepare filling: make the custard, using black coffee in place of milk, and sweeten to taste. Cover the custard to prevent a skin forming and beat thoroughly from time to time as it cools.

Chop remaining walnuts and whip cream until soft. When the coffee mixture is quite cold, fold in half the cream and the walnuts. Stick the small meringues around the edge of the large round, fixing them in position with a little whipped cream. Fill the centre with coffee filling and decorate this with a lattice of piped cream.

Coffee meringue cake

4 egg whites
8 oz caster sugar

For butter cream
4 oz granulated sugar
5 tablespoons water
4 egg yolks
$\frac{3}{4}$ lb unsalted butter
1 teaspoon instant coffee
(dissolved in 2 teaspoons
hot water)

For decoration
3 oz browned almonds (finely
chopped)
2 tablespoons icing sugar

Method

Have ready three baking sheets
lined with non-stick (silicone)
kitchen paper and set oven at
300°F or Mark $\frac{1}{2}$-1. (These are the
best temperatures for electric
and gas ovens, respectively).
    To make meringue: whisk
the egg whites in a bowl until
stiff, add 4 teaspoons of the
measured sugar and continue
whisking for about 30 seconds.
Fold in the remaining sugar
with a metal spoon. Divide the
mixture evenly between the
three tins and spread carefully
into rounds 8-9 inches in diameter. Bake in pre-set oven for
about 50-60 minutes until
meringue is dry and crisp. Leave
to cool.
    To prepare the butter cream ;
dissolve the sugar in the water
over gentle heat, then boil
steadily to the thread (until the
syrup is sticky between your
fingers and thumb and will pull
into a thin thread when cool). It
is not necessary to use a sugar
thermometer for this as a degree
or two either way makes no
difference to butter cream.
    Pour the syrup while still hot

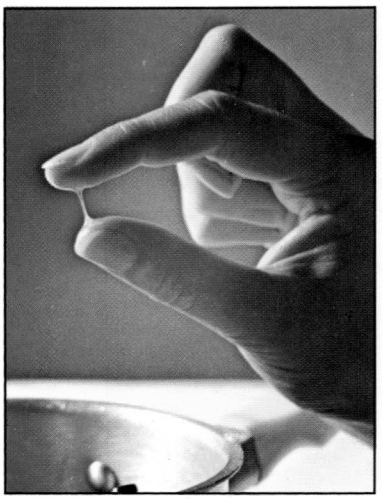

To test sugar syrup : cool a little
on a spoon and **when it is cool** pull
between your finger and thumb
into a fine thread

Pour hot sugar syrup on to egg
yolks, mix to a thick mousse and
beat with creamed butter

56

on to egg yolks, whisk until a thick mousse is formed. Cream the butter until soft and beat in the egg and sugar mousse a little at a time. Add sufficient coffee to give a good flavour.

When the meringue rounds are quite cold spread with some of the coffee butter cream and sandwich them together. Spread the top and sides with remaining butter cream and cover with almonds.

Cut four strips of greaseproof paper 1-inch wide and lay across the top of the cake; the spaces between the strips should be the same. Dust the top of the cake with icing sugar, then carefully lift off each strip of paper.

When the meringue rounds are cold, sandwich together with cream and spread rest on top and sides. Decorate in strips as below

Gâteau Diane

4 egg whites
8 oz caster sugar

For filling
8 oz plain block chocolate
4 fl oz water
1 pint double cream

For decoration
2 oz chocolate caraque

The meringue rounds can be made at least one week before using and stored in airtight tins. They should be packed in layers one on top of the other with a layer of greaseproof paper between each round.

Method

Line 3 baking sheets with non-stick (silicone) kitchen paper; set oven at 250-300°F or Mark $\frac{1}{2}$-1.

Prepare the meringue by beating the egg whites until stiff and adding half the sugar. Whisk mixture until stiff, then fold in the remaining sugar. Spread or pipe the mixture into 3 thin rounds, 8-9 inches in diameter, on the prepared baking sheets. Bake meringues in pre-set cool oven for about 50-60 minutes, or longer, until they are dry and crisp.

To make the filling; break the chocolate into small pieces, put it in a pan with the water and dissolve over very gentle heat. Tip chocolate into a bowl and allow to cool. Whip the cream until it begins to thicken, then add the chocolate and continue beating until it is thick.

To serve; spread each round with the chocolate cream and layer one on top of the other.

Spread the top and sides with the same cream and decorate with the chocolate caraque (see right). The cake must be filled at least 2-3 hours before serving and can be done the day before, providing it is left in the refrigerator overnight. This will keep the meringue soft enough to cut, but the covering of cream by excluding the air will prevent the meringue from becoming too soft.

A slice of the gâteau Diane, made with three meringue rounds spread with chocolate cream, and decorated with chocolate caraque

Chocolate caraque

Grate 2 oz plain chocolate or chocolate couverture (cooking chocolate). Melt it on a plate over a pan of hot water and work with a palette knife until smooth. Spread this thinly on a marble slab or laminated surface and leave until nearly set. Then, using a long sharp knife, shave it off the slab slantwise, using a slight sawing movement and holding the knife almost upright. The chocolate will form long scrolls or flakes. These will keep in an airtight tin but look better when they are freshly made.

Shaving off long scrolls or flakes with a palette knife to make the chocolate caraque

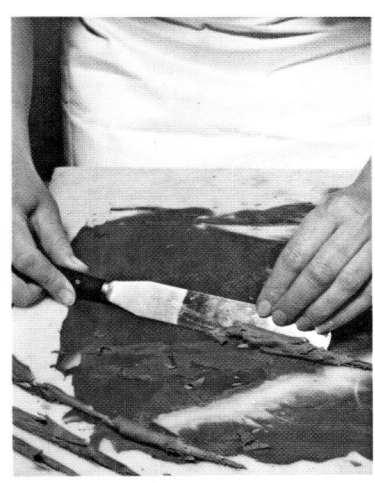

Lemon meringue pie

For rich shortcrust pastry
6 oz plain flour
pinch of salt
3½ oz butter
1 egg yolk
1-2 tablespoons cold water

For filling
1 rounded tablespoon cornflour
½ pint milk
1 rounded tablespoon sugar
2 egg yolks
grated rind and juice of 1 lemon

For meringue
2 egg whites
4 oz caster sugar

7-inch diameter flan ring

Method

Make the rich shortcrust pastry (see method page 17) and set aside to chill. Then line on to the flan ring and bake blind.

Mix the cornflour with a little of the milk in a bowl and heat the rest of the milk in a saucepan. Pour on to the mixed cornflour, return to the pan and boil for 3-4 minutes, stirring continuously to make it smooth. Add the sugar, allow to cool a little, beat in the egg yolks, the grated lemon rind and juice. Pour this mixture into the pastry case; bake for about 10 minutes at 325°F or Mark 3 to set.

To make meringue: whisk the egg whites with a fork or wire whisk until stiff and dry. Whisk in 2 teaspoons of the sugar and then carefully fold in the remainder with a metal spoon. **Watchpoint** Whisking in this small quantity of sugar helps set the whites and folding in the bulk is important to avoid knocking out the air beaten into the whites. If you overstir, the sugar starts to liquefy and the egg whites collapse, resulting in a rather thin layer of meringue which is also tough on the top.

Pile the meringue on the top to cover the filling completely, dredge with caster sugar. To set meringue, place in a cool oven for 10-15 minutes at 275°F or Mark 1. The consistency of a meringue topping should be that of a marshmallow, firm to cut, yet soft and with a crisp coating.

Stuffed apples in meringue
with chocolate sauce

6 large dessert apples
3 tablespoons sugar (dissolved
in ¾ pint water)
1 vanilla pod, or 3-4 drops of
vanilla essence

For mincemeat mixture
4 oz mixed dried fruit
small piece of candied peel
½ oz butter

For meringue
2 egg whites
4 oz caster sugar

For chocolate sauce
2 tablespoons cocoa
1 tablespoon sugar

*Meringue is spooned or piped on
to the cooked apple and then baked.
Chocolate sauce is poured over
apples before serving*

Method
Bring sugar syrup to boil and boil steadily for 10 minutes, flavouring with vanilla. Peel and core apples (a pippin variety such as Cox's or Blenheim is ideal) and poach them carefully in the syrup. To make sure that apples are tender right through, turn them during the cooking time. When tender, remove from the pan with a draining spoon (reserving the syrup) and arrange in ovenproof serving dish.

To prepare the mincemeat: chop the fruit and candied peel and put into a pan with the butter and 1 tablespoon of the syrup in which the apples were cooked. Stir over a gentle heat for 5 minutes, then stuff the mincemeat into cooked apples.

To prepare the meringue: whip the egg whites until stiff, then whisk in 1 tablespoon of the sugar for 1 minute and, using a tablespoon, fold in the remainder carefully. Cover each apple with meringue. This can be done with a spoon, or piped on with a vegetable rose nozzle. Dust with caster sugar and bake for 15-20 minutes until golden-brown in the oven at 275-300°F or Mark 1-2.

To make chocolate sauce: mix cocoa and sugar to a paste with a little of the poaching syrup, add mixture to pan of syrup and simmer gently for 15 minutes. Pour hot sauce round apples before serving.

Vacherin aux marrons

(meringue with chestnut purée filling)

For meringue
4 egg whites
8 oz caster sugar

For filling
1 lb chestnuts
1 vanilla pod
2 tablespoons sugar
4 tablespoons water
$\frac{1}{4}$ pint double cream (whipped)

To decorate
icing sugar
1 oz plain chocolate (grated)

Method

Set oven at 275°F or Mark 1; line two baking sheets with non-stick (silicone) kitchen paper.

Whisk egg whites until stiff in a bowl, add 1 tablespoon of measured sugar and whisk for about 1 minute. Fold in rest of sugar with metal spoon. Divide mixture evenly and spread carefully on to the two baking sheets in two rounds, 8-9 inches in diameter. For a more professional appearance, use a nylon forcing bag fitted with a $\frac{1}{2}$-inch éclair nozzle and pipe meringue in a spiral shape (see photographs below). Bake in the pre-set oven for about 50-60 minutes until lightly-coloured and quite dry. Put on a wire cooling tray, peel off paper, leave to cool.

Meanwhile skin and cook chestnuts with vanilla pod for added flavour and sieve (see page 51). Dissolve sugar in water in a pan, bring to boil,

The uncooked meringue mixture is spread or piped (using a spiral motion) into two rounds on grease-proof paper on the baking sheet

When cooked, meringue halves should be lightly coloured. Cool on a wire rack, then sandwich the halves with chestnut purée

pour carefully into a small bowl
or cup. Leave to cool.

Work the sugar syrup into
chestnut purée. Whip cream,
mix half with chestnut purée.
Use mixture to sandwich together the two meringue rounds.
Dust top with icing sugar, decorate with remaining cream and
grated chocolate.

*Vacherin aux marrons : the finished
meringue*

Meringue topping

For meringue suisse
2 egg whites
**4 oz caster sugar (plus extra for
    dredging)**

This quantity of meringue suisse will be sufficient for a pudding or pie for 4-6 people.

Method
Set oven at 300°F or Mark 2. Make meringue suisse, as in Meringue Chantilly (see page 52) and pile on to the pudding or pie. Dredge with caster sugar and leave for a few minutes before putting in oven.

Cook for about 30 minutes, until the meringue is a delicate brown and crisp on the top. The inside should have the consistency of a marshmallow — white, firm and easy to cut.

Meringue cuite

8½ oz icing sugar
4 egg whites

Method
Sift the icing sugar through a fine sieve and tip it into a basin containing beaten egg whites. Place the basin over a pan of simmering water and whisk the whites and sugar together until thick and holding their shape.

Flavour the meringue and use according to recipe.

Meringue italienne

8 oz lump sugar
6-7 tablespoons water
4 egg whites

Sugar thermometer

Method
First prepare sugar syrup by putting sugar and water in pan ; dissolve sugar over gentle heat and then cook quickly without stirring to 260°F.

Meanwhile beat egg whites until stiff and, when sugar syrup is ready, pour it steadily on to egg whites, mixing quickly with a whisk. Continue whisking until all sugar has been absorbed.

When cold this meringue is used as a topping and / or filling for cakes, or to replace cream.

Note : see also Apricot suédoise, page 138.

Soufflés

Hot soufflés are often considered to be the test of a good cook. They are not difficult to make if you follow the basic rules, but, as with all tests of skill, circumstances must be right. A hot soufflé **must** be served straight from the oven, and it will take about 20-30 minutes to bake. Like a cake mixture, it needs handling lightly and quickly and popping straight into the oven when it is mixed.

When cooked, the top of a soufflé should be evenly brown and firm to the touch. The consistency should be lightly firm, with the centre soft and creamy.

A cold soufflé is a case of gentle deception. Being a cold mixture, lightly set with gelatine, it cannot rise; but it is always presented in the conventional soufflé dish, prepared so that the finished soufflé will stand above the dish, as if it had risen.

For a cold sweet soufflé, the eggs are always separated, the yolks are beaten with the sugar and flavouring (in the form of juice or purée) until thick, or made into a custard with milk when cream is added. Stiffly-whisked egg whites are folded in to give it the characteristic soufflé texture, and the whole is lightly set with gelatine.

Rules for making hot soufflés

1 Choose the right size soufflé dish or case for the quantity of mixture being made. Dishes are generally numbered 1-3, and the equivalent diameter tops are 7 inches (No. 1), 6 inches (No. 2) and $5\frac{1}{2}$ inches (No. 3).

2 Prepare the dish by rubbing the inside lightly with butter.

3 To allow the soufflé to rise 2-3 inches above the dish when baked, cut a band of doubled greaseproof paper, about 6-7 inches wide, and long enough to overlap some 3 inches round side of dish. Make a 2-inch fold along one long side. Butter the strip above this fold, and wrap the band round the outside of the dish, the folded piece at the base and turned inwards. This will keep the paper upright and firm. The greased section of the paper should stand above dish by some 3 inches.

Tying paper band round to stand 2-3 inches above rim of the dish

bowl and a light wire whisk. Whisking by hand in a bowl of this shape (see photograph below) gives more bulk to the whites. If you do not have a copper bowl, use a wire whisk with a china or earthenware bowl. Don't use a rotary whisk or electric mixer.

5 When adding egg whites to the mixture, stir in a small quantity with a metal spoon before the main bulk is added. This first addition softens the mixture so that once the remaining whites are added the whole remains light and fluffy.

6 Pre-heat the oven to 375°F or Mark 5. Arrange the shelves so that the soufflé can be placed in the centre of the oven, with no shelf above it. This will give it plenty of room to rise. To avoid any unnecessary opening of oven door, try not to cook anything else when a soufflé is in.

7 Hot soufflés benefit by the addition of 1 extra white to yolks. Though this is not essential, it makes for a lighter and fluffier mixture.

Tie paper securely with string and set the dish on a baking sheet before filling. The string should be untied and the paper peeled off just before serving.

4 It is the whipped egg whites that make a soufflé rise, so it is important to whip them well. Ideally you should use a copper

A little of the egg white is first folded in to soften the mixture

Orange, or lemon, soufflé

3 oz lump sugar (about 18 lumps)
2 oranges, or lemons
$\frac{1}{2}$ pint milk
1 rounded tablespoon flour
1 oz butter
3 egg yolks
4 egg whites
little sifted icing sugar

7-inch diameter top (No. 1 size) soufflé dish

Method
Prepare soufflé dish. Set oven at 375°F or Mark 5.

For orange soufflé, rub some of the lumps of sugar over the outside rind of the oranges until they are soaked with the oil (zest). Then set aside.

Mix 3 tablespoons of the milk with the flour until smooth. Scald remaining milk, add all the sugar lumps (and grated lemon rind if using) and cover. Leave to infuse for 5-7 minutes off the heat. Then return pan to heat. Add the flour mixture gradually and stir until boiling. Boil 2-3 seconds, then draw aside and dot the surface with the butter. Cover and leave for 5 minutes.

Beat in egg yolks, one at a time. Whip whites to a firm snow, stir in 1 tablespoon, then cut and stir in remainder, using a metal spoon. Turn at once into prepared dish and bake in pre-set oven for about 18-20 minutes or until well risen.

Then draw out oven shelf with soufflé on it, dust top quickly with icing sugar and return shelf. Cook for a further 4-5 minutes to caramelise the top. Serve at once.

Gooseberry soufflé

$\frac{1}{2}$ pint gooseberry purée (made with 1 lb green gooseberries, $\frac{1}{4}$ pint water, 4 rounded tablespoons granulated sugar, 4-5 heads of elderflowers)
4 eggs (separated)
2 oz caster sugar
$\frac{1}{4}$ pint double cream
$\frac{1}{2}$ oz gelatine
5 tablespoons water
2-3 drops of green colouring (optional)

For decoration
7 fl oz double cream (whipped)
browned almonds (finely chopped), or crushed ratafia crumbs

6-inch diameter top (No. 2 size) soufflé dish

Method
Tie a band of oiled greaseproof paper around the outside of the dish.

Beat egg yolks, sugar and purée in a bowl. Whisk mixture over heat until it is thick, then remove from heat and continue whisking until bowl is cool (heat is not necessary if using an electric mixer).

Half whip the $\frac{1}{4}$ pint cream, stir into gooseberry mixture. Soak gelatine in water, then dissolve over gentle heat; add to soufflé with colouring. When mixture begins to thicken, whisk egg whites to a firm snow, fold in carefully and turn soufflé into dish; leave it to set.

Decorate with whipped cream and the nuts or ratafia crumbs.

Remove the greaseproof paper before serving.

Orange soufflé nantaise

4 tablespoons crushed macaroons
little Grand Marnier liqueur
3 large eggs (separated)
6 oz caster sugar
grated rind of 1 lemon
grated rind and strained juice of
   3 small oranges
$\frac{1}{2}$ pint double cream
$\frac{1}{2}$ oz gelatine
juice of $\frac{1}{2}$ lemon (made up to
   $2\frac{1}{2}$ fl oz with water)

For decoration
1 small carton ($2\frac{1}{2}$ fl oz) double
   cream (whipped and sweetened)
2 tablespoons macaroon crumbs

*6-inch diameter top (No. 2 size)
soufflé dish*

Method

Prepare soufflé dish; soak the macaroons in the liqueur.

Place the egg yolks, sugar, lemon and orange rinds and strained orange juice together in a basin over hot water and whisk over gentle heat until the mixture is thick and mousse-like. Remove from the heat and continue whisking for 5 minutes or until the bowl is cool.

Lightly whip cream and fold it into the mixture. Dissolve the gelatine in the lemon juice and water and stir this liquid into the mixture. Whisk the egg whites until stiff but not dry, set bowl of soufflé mixture on ice and fold in egg whites. As the mixture begins to thicken, turn it into the soufflé dish, layering it with the macaroons; put in a cool place to set.

When firm, remove the paper from the soufflé dish, press the macaroon crumbs gently round the sides and decorate the top of the soufflé with rosettes of whipped, sweetened cream, or as left.

Baked vanilla soufflé

1 vanilla pod, or $\frac{1}{2}$ teaspoon vanilla essence
$\frac{1}{2}$ pint milk
2 rounded tablespoons caster sugar
1 tablespoon flour
1 dessertspoon arrowroot
1 oz butter
3 egg yolks
4 egg whites
little sifted icing sugar

7-inch diameter top (No. 1 size) soufflé dish

Method

Reserve 4 tablespoons of the milk. If using vanilla pod, infuse it in the remaining milk. Prepare soufflé dish; set oven at 375°F or Mark 5.

Bring the milk to the boil, add the sugar and vanilla essence (if using), cover and draw aside. Blend the reserved milk with the flour and arrowroot, add to the pan of milk, return to the heat and stir until boiling. Boil for 2-3 seconds, then draw aside, dot with the butter, cover and leave for 5 minutes. Then stir to mix in butter and beat in yolks one at a time. Whip whites to a firm snow, and cut and fold into the mixture.

Turn into the soufflé dish and bake in pre-set oven for 20 minutes. Dust the top with icing sugar and put back in the oven for 4-5 minutes to caramelise the top.

Soufflé moka praline

For praline
2 oz almonds (unblanched)
2 oz caster sugar

4 eggs
4 oz caster sugar
2 dessertspoons instant coffee
(dissolved in 6 tablespoons
boiling water)
$\frac{1}{2}$ pint double cream
$\frac{1}{2}$ oz gelatine
5 tablespoons cold water

*6-inch diameter top (No. 2 size)
soufflé dish*

Method

First prepare the praline: place the almonds and sugar in a small heavy saucepan and dissolve sugar over gentle heat. As the sugar turns brown, stir the mixture carefully until the almonds are toasted on all sides. Turn mixture on to an oiled tin, slab or plate. When cold, crush praline with a rolling pin or pass through a nut mill or mincer.

Prepare the dish. Separate the eggs and place the yolks, sugar and dissolved coffee in a basin and whisk over heat until thick and mousse-like (or use electric beater without heat). Remove soufflé mixture from the heat and continue whisking until the bowl is cold.

Lightly whip the cream and fold about two-thirds into the mixture. Soak the gelatine in the water and then dissolve it over heat; add this to the

Whisking egg yolks, sugar and coffee together until thick

Piping whipped cream round the top of soufflé moka praline

mixture. Whisk the egg whites until stiff and fold into the soufflé with 2 oz of the praline. Stir it carefully until it begins to thicken, then turn into the prepared dish and leave to set.

When soufflé is set, remove the paper and decorate the top with the remaining whipped cream and the praline.

Soufflé moka praline, decorated with crushed praline and cream

Chocolate soufflé

4 oz plain chocolate (cut in small pieces)
2 tablespoons water
$\frac{1}{2}$ pint milk
2 rounded tablespoons caster sugar
2-3 drops of vanilla essence
1 tablespoon flour
1 dessertspoon arrowroot
1 oz butter
3 egg yolks
4 egg whites
little sifted icing sugar

7-inch diameter top (No. 1 size) soufflé dish

Method

Prepare the soufflé dish. Set oven at 375°F or Mark 5.

Cut up the chocolate into very small pieces, put into a medium-size pan with the water and stir over slow heat until melted. Add the milk, reserving 4 tablespoons.

Bring milk and chocolate to the boil, add sugar and vanilla, cover pan and draw aside.

Blend the reserved milk with the flour and arrowroot, pour this into the chocolate, return to the heat and bring to the boil, stirring all the time. Boil for 2-3 seconds, then draw aside, dot the surface with small pieces of butter, cover and leave for 5 minutes. Then stir to mix in the butter thoroughly and beat in yolks one at a time.

Whip whites to a firm snow, cut and stir 1 tablespoon into the mixture, using a metal spoon, then stir in the rest.

Turn mixture into the prepared soufflé dish and bake in pre-set oven for 20 minutes.

Pull out oven shelf with soufflé on it, dust the top with sifted icing sugar and put soufflé back for 4-5 minutes to caramelise the top. Serve at once.

Pancakes

Pancakes are traditionally Shrove Tuesday fare. All over the world, Christians feast and carnival before the Lenten fast, and rich, delicious pancakes are one of the favourite ways of using up butter, eggs and milk that won't be needed in Lent. In England we no longer celebrate in the streets, but our Pancake Day remains.

At other times of the year, pancakes are a particular delight to the extrovert cook — cooked in a chafing dish beside the table and served flaming from the pan, they make an occasion of any meal.

Pancakes don't have to be made and served at once. Not only the batter, but the pancakes themselves, can be made several hours or even the day before they are wanted. For this, however, the batter must contain a good proportion of eggs and melted butter. If pancakes are kept in an airtight container and reheated properly, they taste as if fresh-cooked from the pan.

The right pan is most important for making pancakes. It should be small, with a base of about 6 inches in diameter and made of cast iron or aluminium. A proper pancake pan is shallow (the sides about $\frac{3}{4}$ inch high) to make the tossing easier. These pans are not easy to come by and you can use an omelet pan (which has a curved edge) instead, but choose a shallow rather than a deep one.

Ideally it is better to keep the pan entirely for making pancakes and omelets, as in either case it is better not to wash it after use unless really necessary.

The pan should be well wiped with a damp cloth or paper dipped in salt, then rubbed lightly with a few drops of oil. It can then be put away for future use. This treatment helps to prevent sticking.

A good pancake should be wafer-thin with a crisp lacy edge. Butter or oil in the batter gives this effect, so little or no fat is necessary in the pan.

To cook pancakes. Once the batter is made it must be allowed to stand before use. To cook the pancakes, wipe out the pan before setting over moderate heat. When thoroughly hot put in a few drops of oil. Take 1 tablespoon of the batter and tip this into the pan, immediately rolling it round clockwise to coat the bottom evenly. (This quantity will be sufficient for a 6-inch diameter pan.)

Cook until the underneath of pancake is a good brown colour. Run a palette knife under the edges to loosen the pancake, then raise it slightly with the fingers and slip the knife underneath. Flip the pancake over and cook for about 10 seconds on the other side. Alternatively toss the pancakes. Then turn them on to a rack. Continue to cook pancakes, stacking them one on top of the other, until you have as many as you want. Cover the stack with a bowl or wrap in a tea towel if not for immediate use. If they are for use the following day, store in foil or a polythene bag with a sheet of greaseproof, or waxed, paper between each pancake.

To reheat pancakes. Melt about 1 oz of butter, brush a baking sheet or tray with this, then peel off the pancakes and lay them overlapping along the sheet. Brush well with more melted butter to exclude the air and protect pancakes during cooking.

Put baking sheet into the oven at 400°F or Mark 6 for 3-4 minutes. Do this for pancakes without a stuffing, otherwise stuff them while cold and bake them with the stuffing in for 7-10 minutes.

If all the batter is not used, keep it covered and use within three days.

Basic pancake batter

4 oz plain flour
pinch of salt
1 egg
1 egg yolk
½ pint milk
1 tablespoon melted butter, or
  salad oil

Method

Sift the flour with the salt into a bowl, make a well in the centre, add the egg and yolk and begin to add the milk slowly, stirring all the time. When half the milk has been added, stir in the melted butter or oil and beat well until smooth.

Add the remaining milk and leave to stand for 30 minutes before using. The batter should have the consistency of thin cream — if too thick, add a little extra milk.

Allow two pancakes per person.

Apricot pancakes

1 lb apricots (stoned)
sugar syrup (made with $\frac{1}{2}$ pint
    water, 3 rounded tablespoons
    granulated sugar, and pared
    rind of $\frac{1}{2}$ lemon)
2 tablespoons apricot jam (sieved)
juice of $\frac{1}{2}$ lemon
2 tablespoons almonds (flaked and
    browned)

For pancake batter
4 oz plain flour
pinch of salt
1 egg
1 egg yolk
$\frac{1}{2}$ pint milk
2 tablespoons salad oil, or melted
    butter

6-inch diameter base heavy frying pan

Method

Make the sugar syrup and poach apricots in it (see method, page 30).

To prepare the pancake batter: sift flour with salt into a bowl, add egg and egg yolk and gradually stir in half the milk. Beat well and add half the oil or butter, then whisk in remaining milk. Let the batter stand for 30 minutes before frying small, paper-thin pancakes.

To fry pancakes: heat pan and add 2-3 drops of oil or melted butter. Pour 1 tablespoon of batter into pan, immediately rolling it around clockwise to coat the bottom evenly. Cook pancake until underneath is golden-brown, then toss or flip over and cook for a further 1-2 seconds. Cook remaining batter in same way.

Stack the pancakes on top of each other on a cake rack until wanted. If they are to be kept for a few hours or overnight, wrap in a tea towel. Alternatively the pancakes can be wrapped in aluminium foil or a polythene bag. Lift the apricots from the pan with a draining spoon, add the jam and lemon juice to the apricot syrup, stir over a gentle heat until the jam has melted, then boil for about 5 minutes until thick and syrupy. Strain.

Layer the pancakes with the apricots in a buttered ovenproof dish, starting and finishing with a pancake. Cut like a cake into individual portions and pour over the sauce.

Bake in oven at 400°F or Mark 6 for about 10 minutes, until brown and crisp. Scatter almonds on top and serve hot.

Pancakes à la crème

½ pint pancake batter (see page 74)

For pastry cream
1 egg (separated)
1 egg yolk
2 oz caster sugar
¾ oz flour
½ oz cornflour
½ pint milk
1 piece of vanilla pod, or strip of
  lemon, or orange, rind

For topping
1-2 tablespoons icing sugar
1 oz almonds (finely shredded)

Method
Prepare batter, leave to stand in a cool place for 30 minutes.

To prepare the pastry cream: cream both egg yolks with 1 oz sugar until white. Add the flour and cornflour and mix with a little of the milk until smooth.

Heat the remaining milk with the vanilla pod or rind and tip on to the egg mixture. Return this mixture to pan, stir over a gentle heat until boiling.

Watchpoint It is very important to use gentle heat or the eggs will curdle before the flour is cooked.

Whisk the egg white and remaining sugar together until thick, then stir this into the hot custard. Set aside and keep warm in a bain-marie.

Fry paper-thin pancakes, spread each one with pastry cream, fold them in three and arrange on a hot buttered serving dish. Dust thickly with icing sugar before marking on a pattern with red hot skewers (heat several at once under the grill or in a flame while frying the pancakes). Scatter with almonds and serve very hot.

Creole pancakes

For batter
3 oz flour
pinch of salt
2 eggs
5-7½ fl oz milk
1 tablespoon butter (melted), or
  olive oil
4 tablespoons crushed
  macaroons
kirsch

For finishing
1 pineapple (fresh), or 1 large can
sugar syrup (see page 39)
2-3 tablespoons apricot jam
little extra melted butter
icing sugar (for dusting)

Method
Make the batter, reserving 1 egg white, and leave in a cool place for about 1 hour. Just before frying pancakes, whisk the egg white until stiff and fold into the batter with the macaroon crumbs and a little kirsch. Fry the pancakes and stack one on top of the other.

Set oven at 425°F or Mark 7.

Dice the pineapple, heat quickly in a pan with a little sugar syrup and add the apricot jam and kirsch to taste. Place a tablespoon of pineapple on each pancake, fold them in three and place in a warm buttered ovenproof dish.

Brush pancakes with a little extra melted butter, dust with icing sugar and put into the preset oven for 2-3 minutes.

To serve, pour 2-3 tablespoons kirsch into the hot dish and set it alight.

Pancakes with maple syrup

6 oz superfine flour (sifted)
$1\frac{1}{2}$ teaspoons baking powder
1 teaspoon caster sugar
large pinch of salt
1 egg
7-8 fl oz milk
1 oz butter (melted)

In Canada these are eaten for breakfast with crispy fried bacon. This quantity makes 12-16 pancakes.

Method
Sift the flour into a mixing bowl with the baking powder, sugar and salt. Beat the egg very well, add the milk to it and then add this mixture to the flour with the melted butter and beat well until really smooth. (A rotary beater is best for this.) Beat for at least 3 minutes until bubbles break freely over the surface.

Fry the pancakes on a heavy girdle until golden-brown on each side. The girdle should be heated while the batter is being made and to test if it is hot enough sprinkle it with a few drops of cold water. The bubbles should dance around if the heat is right and the pancakes will brown immediately. **Note :** the pancakes can be made thick or thin just as you like and it is quite easy to adjust the batter by adding a little extra milk if you like your pancakes really thin.

Turn the pancakes as soon as they are puffy and full of bubbles but it is most important, if the pancakes are to be really light, that you turn them before these bubbles break.

Serve them in stacks of 3-4 per person with pats of unsalted butter and a jug of maple syrup.

Pancakes sultane

For batter
$4\frac{1}{2}$ oz flour
pinch of salt
1 oz caster sugar
2 eggs
$7\frac{1}{2}$ fl oz milk
1 tablespoon melted butter
2 tablespoons double cream
1 tablespoon rum (optional)
1 macaroon (crushed and sieved)

For filling
2 bananas
4 slices fresh, or canned, pineapple
4 tablespoons apricot jam

To finish
2 tablespoons icing sugar (sifted)
2 tablespoons rum

Method
Prepare pancake batter as basic recipe (see page 74), adding cream with the butter. Leave for 30 minutes in a cool place.

Stir in the rum and macaroon crumbs just before frying.

Cut the bananas in rather thick slanting slices and quarter the rings of pineapple. Bind the fruit together with apricot jam.

Set the oven at 425°F or Mark 7. Fry very thin pancakes, spread each with the fruit mixture and fold in four — first sides to middle and then in half. Arrange, overlapping, in a buttered ovenproof dish and dust with the icing sugar. Slip into the pre-set oven for 3-5 minutes. Pour rum into the dish and set alight, serve at once.

Crêpes Suzette

For batter
3 oz flour
pinch of salt
1 egg
1 egg yolk
1 tablespoon olive oil, or 2 tablespoons clarified butter
1 dessertspoon orange curaçao
7½ fl oz milk

For orange butter
6-8 lumps of sugar
2 oranges
2 oz butter
1 tablespoon orange curaçao

For serving
little extra melted butter
icing sugar (for dusting)
2-3 tablespoons brandy, or rum
  (for flaming)

Removing zest from oranges by rubbing over sugar lumps

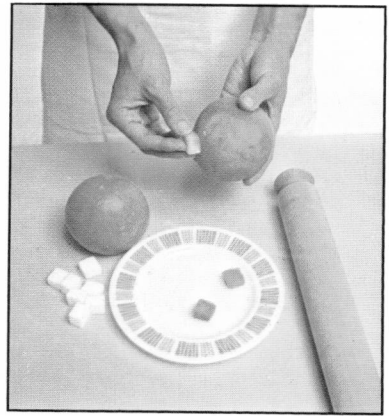

Method

Make the batter (see method, page 74), adding curaçao at the same time as the eggs and oil or butter. Leave to stand in a cool place for at least 30 minutes before using.

Meanwhile make the orange butter: rub each lump of sugar on the skin of the oranges to remove zest. As you do this the sugar will become saturated with the oil in the zest, and the oranges will look quite bald. Crush the sugar, preferably in a mortar, then work in the creamed butter and curaçao. If you haven't a pestle and mortar, this can be done with the end of your rolling pin in a pudding basin. Keep in a cool place until wanted.

Note : this old-fashioned way of preparing the orange butter is still the very best and perhaps explains why crêpes Suzette are always expensive on a menu.

Fry the pancakes as thinly as possible. As the batter is very rich, containing extra butter and liqueur, it is possible to fry them extra thin so that they look quite lacy.

If entertaining at home, the most practical and the simplest way of serving is as follows: set the oven at 300°F or Mark 2, brush a baking tin with a little butter, spread out the pancakes, overlapping each other rather like a pack of cards, and brush with butter. Put pancakes into the pre-set oven for about 5 minutes only.

Have ready a warm serving dish, spread each pancake with orange butter, then fold in three. The folding is traditional — in three like a tricorne (right). Arrange pancakes, overlapping, down the dish and dust with icing sugar. Return them to the oven while the main course is being eaten. Just before carrying the dish to the dining table, heat the brandy or rum in a small pan, set alight and pour over the pancakes.

Adding pre-cooked pancake to foaming butter in chafing dish

Turning and folding pancake before lifting out of the dish

To flame pancakes :

If you have a chafing dish and a husband who would love to take over the finishing touch at the dining table, this is what you do to flame pancakes.

Just before serving dinner, unwrap the pancakes you made earlier in the day (it doesn't matter if they are cold) and spread each one with orange butter. (This should be done on the underside, ie. the side fried last, as it never looks as nice and should always become the inside of the filled pancake.)

Stack the pancakes on a plate, put this on a tray with the bottle of brandy or rum, a sherry glass, palette knife, fork, tablespoon and $\frac{1}{2}$ oz unsalted butter. Put this tray beside the chafing dish and have ready a hot serving dish.

Your husband can then carry on as follows : drop butter in the pan and, when foaming, rotate the pan so the whole surface is lightly coated ; put in a pancake, orange butter side down, turn and fold in three ; then lift on to the hot dish.

He should continue in this way until all the pancakes have been heated and turned in their orange butter. By the time the last few pancakes have been heated the sauce should be caramelising on the bottom of the pan — this will give a superb flavour. Then pour the brandy first into the glass and then into the pan. Swill it around pan, tilt and allow brandy to ignite (from the flame). Pour the sauce, while flaming, over the pancakes and serve them at once.

Crêpes Suzette (continued)

Crêpes Suzette set in a serving dish after flaming with brandy

Pancakes Longueville

For batter
4 oz flour
pinch of salt
1 oz caster sugar
1 egg
1 egg yolk
grated rind of 1 orange
2 tablespoons melted butter
scant ½ pint milk
1 oz almonds (freshly blanched and finely chopped) — see page 13

For filling
6 dessert apples (pippin)
grated rind and juice of ½ lemon and ½ orange
4 tablespoons smooth apricot jam
1 small carton (2½ fl oz) double cream
¼ teaspoon cinnamon

To finish
1 tablespoon melted butter
2 tablespoons icing sugar (sifted)

Method
Prepare pancake batter as basic recipe (see page 74), adding grated orange rind with the egg. Leave for 30 minutes in a cool place.

Don't add almonds until just before frying the pancakes.

For filling: peel, quarter and remove the core of the apples and then cut in thick slices. Put in a pan with the lemon and orange rind and juice and the jam, cover and cook until thick and pulpy. Whip the cream and flavour with the cinnamon.

Set the oven at 425°F or Mark 7. When the pancakes are fried fold the cream into the apple mixture. Spread each pancake with the filling, fold in four and place overlapping in a buttered ovenproof dish. Brush with the melted butter, dust with icing sugar and glaze in the pre-set oven for 3-5 minutes.

Praline pancakes

½ pint pancake batter (as basic recipe, page 74)
2 oz butter
1½ oz caster sugar
2 tablespoons praline powder
rum

These pancakes are good served with pêches flambées — peaches poached in syrup — drained of all but 1 tablespoon of juice, and flamed with brandy or rum.

Method
Prepare batter and leave to stand for 30 minutes. Cream butter, beat in the sugar gradually and when white and thick mix in the praline powder and flavour well with rum.

Fry pancakes. Quickly spread each with praline butter, roll up, and reheat quickly in oven at 400°F or Mark 6. Serve at once.

Praline powder
This can be made ahead of time and stored in an airtight container: for about 5 tablespoons powder put 3 oz of unblanched almonds and 3 oz caster sugar into a pan. Set on a low heat until sugar melts. When it is turning a pale, golden-brown, stir with a metal spoon and continue cooking until it is nut-brown. Turn on to an oiled tin, slab or plate and leave until hard. Then crush into coarse powder with a rolling pin or use a nut mill, mincer or grinder, or pound to a paste.

Apple pancakes

½ pint pancake batter (as basic recipe, page 74) — with 1 teaspoon sugar added with oil

For filling
1½-2 lb apples (peeled, cored and sliced)
½ oz butter
brown sugar
cinnamon
lemon rind

For apricot sauce
4 tablespoons smooth apricot jam
grated rind and juice of 1 lemon
½ pint water
1 teaspoon arrowroot

Method
Make batter and leave in a cool place for about 30 minutes.

Peel, core and slice the apples, rub the butter over the bottom of a thick pan, put in the apples with sugar to taste, cinnamon and lemon rind. Cover and cook slowly until tender but not too mushy, about 10-15 minutes.

Place the jam, juice and rind of the lemon and the water in a pan and dissolve over gentle heat. Mix the arrowroot with a little water, add to the pan and stir until boiling. Cook for 2-3 minutes until clear, then strain.

Fry the pancakes wafer-thin. Stack them on an ovenproof dish, one above the other, sandwiching them with the apple mixture (below). Spoon over some apricot sauce and bake in the oven at 375°F or Mark 5, until lightly brown (about 10 minutes). Cut into wedges, pour more apricot sauce round, and serve remainder separately.

Milk puddings and creams

No one has to be told that milk is a staple diet. It contains protein, calcium and vitamins in high proportions, and it is for this reason that milk is so highly recommended for children, expectant mothers and invalids. With so much emphasis laid on its nutritive value, one is apt to lose sight of the fact that milk is also delicious — whether drunk on its own, in other beverages, or cooked as a sauce or even a main dish at a meal.

Few people are fully aware of the variety of sweets that can be made with milk. Creamy, slip-down-your-throat desserts, rich, thick custards on their own or with fruit, pastries or puddings ; light or rich, for entertaining, feeding an invalid or stoking a hungry family, milk puddings are among the easiest and best.

Made with cereals — rice, barley, sago, or semolina — milk puddings are baked in a slow oven until soft and creamy, with a golden-brown skin. To get the best results, the milk used should be rich and creamy. For custards the basic ingredients are eggs and milk used in varying proportions, with different flavours according to the recipe.

Custards play an important part in cooking. They not only form the basis of many sweets and some savoury dishes, but also accompany cooked fruit and hot puddings.

There are two types of custard. The first is when eggs and milk are mixed together and baked, or steamed, to set to a firm consistency, eg. as for caramel custard. The second type of custard is when egg yolks and milk are cooked over a gentle heat to a creamy consistency. This is a soft custard and forms the basis of cold creams and soufflés set with gelatine.

Important points to note

Egg whites will set a custard and egg yolks will give it a creamy consistency. For a cooked custard, eg. baked or steamed, the proportion of eggs to milk should be 2 whole eggs and 2 egg yolks to 1 pint milk. For a soft custard, take 4 egg yolks to 1 pint of milk. More yolks can be added if a very rich custard is called for. Whites tend to curdle the mixture.

Eggs and milk will curdle if allowed to get too hot. For baking a custard in the oven, it is wise to use a bain-marie. This protects the mixture from the direct oven heat. Unless you want to brown the top, eg. for a custard pudding, cover the dish in the bain-marie with a piece of foil, or buttered grease-proof paper, while cooking.

For a soft custard, scald the milk by bringing up to boiling point. You can use a double saucepan, the lower pan containing the hot water, but if care is taken, the custard can be thickened on direct heat. 1 teaspoon of cornflour can replace 1 egg yolk in custard.

Rice pudding

1 pint creamy milk
1 tablespoon ($\frac{3}{4}$ oz) thick grain
  rice
2 tablespoons cold water
$\frac{1}{2}$ oz butter
1 dessertspoon sugar
pinch of nutmeg (optional)

Pie dish (1$\frac{1}{2}$ pints capacity)

Barley and sago puddings are cooked the same way.

Method
Wash the rice and put in the bottom of the pie dish. Add the cold water and leave it to soak for 1 hour. Set oven at 300°F or Mark 2. Drain any water off the rice and pour on the milk. Add butter, sugar and nutmeg. Cook in the pre-set slow oven for 2$\frac{1}{2}$-3 hours. After the first hour, or when a skin just begins to form, stir with a fork. Then leave without stirring until the skin is golden-brown and the rice and milk thick and creamy. If the pudding is still sloppy 30-40 minutes before it is to be eaten, raise the oven temperature to 325°F or Mark 3. Serve hot or cold.

If you intend to serve the pudding cold, take it out of the oven when it is still lightly creamy, as it will become stiffer on cooling.

Semolina pudding

1 pint milk
3 tablespoons semolina (coarse,
  or fine)
$\frac{1}{2}$ oz butter
1 egg (separated)
pinch of grated nutmeg,
  or lemon rind
1 dessertspoon sugar
caster sugar (for sprinkling)

Pie dish (1$\frac{1}{2}$ pints capacity)

Method
Set oven at 350°F or Mark 4. Heat the milk, stir in the semolina and cook over gentle heat, stirring occasionally, for 5-6 minutes. Draw pan aside and add the butter, egg yolk, nutmeg (or lemon rind) and sugar. Whisk the egg white until stiff and fold it into the mixture.

Turn pudding into a buttered ovenproof dish and sprinkle the top with caster sugar. Cook in pre-set moderate oven for 15-20 minutes until the top of the pudding is lightly browned and slightly puffy.

Cold semolina cream

$1\frac{1}{2}$ pints milk
4 tablespoons semolina
1 tablespoon caster sugar
$\frac{1}{2}$ oz butter
grated rind of $\frac{1}{2}$ lemon
2 eggs (separated)

Ring mould ($1\frac{1}{2}$-2 pints capacity)

Method
Rinse out the mould with cold water. Heat the milk gently, shake in the semolina and sugar and cook, stirring occasionally, until the mixture is creamy (it should just drop from the spoon). This process should take about 6-7 minutes.

Then draw pan aside, add the butter, lemon rind and egg yolks. Whisk the egg whites stiffly, then cut and fold them into the cream and pour it into the prepared mould.

Leave semolina cream in a cool place to set, then turn out and serve with either a cold jam sauce, or home-made jam such as strawberry or raspberry.

Watchpoint The semolina cream should pour well from the pan into the mould; if it is too stiff, stir in a little cold milk.

Mecca cream

$7\frac{1}{2}$ fl oz milk
2-3 drops of vanilla essence, or $\frac{1}{2}$ split vanilla pod
$2\frac{1}{2}$ oz butter
$3\frac{1}{2}$ oz plain flour
2 large eggs
1 oz almonds (blanched and shredded) — see page 13
icing sugar (for dusting)
apricot jam sauce (see page 150)

8-inch diameter ovenproof pie plate, or pie dish (1 pint capacity)

Method
First butter the pie plate or dish well; set oven at 400°F or Mark 6.

Put the milk in a pan with the vanilla essence (or pod) and bring it slowly to the boil; remove the vanilla pod, if using, and add the butter. When milk is bubbling, draw pan aside and pour in the flour all at once. Beat the mixture until it is smooth, then leave it to cool.

Beat the eggs in, one at a time, and when the mixture is shiny-looking turn it into the prepared pie plate or dish and scatter the almonds over the top. Bake the cream in pre-set hot oven for 40-45 minutes or until well risen and firm to the touch.

Five minutes before it is cooked, dust with icing sugar and replace in oven to glaze. Serve hot with the apricot jam sauce (page 150).

Norwegian cream

¾ pint milk
2 tablespoons apricot jam
3 eggs (one separated)
1 tablespoon sugar
½ teaspoon vanilla essence
3 tablespoons double cream
   (whipped)

To finish
block chocolate (for caraque, and
   grated for decoration)

*6-inch diameter top (No. 2 size)
soufflé dish*

Method
Spread the apricot jam over the
bottom of the dish. Set oven at
350°F or Mark 4.

Break 2 whole eggs into a
bowl, add 1 egg yolk and cream
with the sugar and vanilla. Heat
the milk and pour it on to this
mixture, blend, strain into dish.

Stand the dish in a roasting
tin half-full of water, cover with
a piece of greaseproof paper
and cook in pre-set moderate
oven for about 45-50 minutes
until firm to the touch. Leave
the cream until cold.

Whip the remaining egg white
stiffly and fold into the whipped
cream. Cover the custard with
the chocolate caraque and pile
the cream on top. Decorate with
more caraque or grated chocolate.

To make chocolate caraque,
see page 59.

Rice cream Tyrolhof

1 pint milk
3 tablespoons thick grain rice
sugar (to taste)
scant $\frac{1}{2}$ oz gelatine
2-3 tablespoons orange juice,
   or water
1 large dessert apple
2-3 tablespoons double cream
   (lightly whipped)

For decoration
double cream
$\frac{1}{2}$ oz almonds

Ring mould (1$\frac{1}{2}$ pints capacity)

Method
Lightly oil the mould. Simmer rice in milk for 35-40 minutes or until tender, stirring occasionally. Draw pan aside, add the sugar and then leave to cool. The consistency must be thick but not too solid, so add a little more milk, if necessary.

Soak gelatine in orange juice (or water), then dissolve it over gentle heat. Peel, core and dice the apple and add to the rice. Stir in the gelatine mixture and, when on the point of setting, fold in the cream. Turn into the mould to set.

Blanch, split and shred the almonds and roast them until a golden-brown in a hot oven.

Turn out the rice and decorate with the cream, scatter over the almonds. Serve with apricot sauce (page 150).

Oatmeal cream

$\frac{3}{4}$ pint milk
$\frac{1}{2}$ cup medium oatmeal
1 large egg (beaten)
grated rind and juice of $\frac{1}{2}$ lemon
1-2 tablespoons caster sugar
   (to taste)
scant $\frac{1}{2}$ oz gelatine
2 tablespoons water
1 small carton (2$\frac{1}{2}$ fl oz) double
   cream (lightly whipped)

Method
Soak the oatmeal in the milk for 30 minutes, turn it into a pan and stir until it is boiling. Then simmer for 3-4 minutes. Pour mixture into a bowl and add the beaten egg, grated lemon rind and sugar to taste.

Dissolve gelatine in the lemon juice and water, add to the mixture when it is cool and then fold in the cream.

Pour the cream into a glass bowl and leave to set. Serve with 3-4 tablespoons of fruit sauce over the top (see pages 150-152).

Riz à l'impératrice

3½ oz thick grain rice
¾ pint milk
drop of vanilla essence
2 oz sugar
scant 1 oz butter
4 oz glacé fruits
2 tablespoons kirsch
½ pint double cream
redcurrant, or apricot, sauce
  (flavoured with kirsch) —
  see page 150

For crème anglaise
4 egg yolks
2 oz sugar
scant 8 fl oz milk
scant ½ oz gelatine (softened in
  1 tablespoon water)

Decorative mould (2 pints capacity)

Whipped cream and glacé fruit are folded into the rice mixture to make the riz à l'impératrice

Method
Lightly grease the mould.

Put the rice into cold water, bring to the boil and cook for 2 minutes. Drain well, and return to the pan with the milk and vanilla and cook at a gentle heat, stirring occasionally to prevent sticking, until the rice is tender and the milk absorbed. Add the sugar and butter.

Meanwhile, prepare the crème anglaise; cream the yolks in a bowl with the sugar, bring the milk to scalding point and pour it over the yolks, then add the gelatine. Stir until gelatine is dissolved and strain.

Cut the fruits into small dice and macerate in the kirsch. When the rice is cold add the custard. Lightly whip the cream and fold into the rice mixture with the glacé fruits, then turn it into lightly greased decorative mould, cover and set on ice or put in the refrigerator to set. For serving turn it on to a cold plate and pour round the redcurrant (or apricot) sauce (see page 150).

Chocolate and caramel rice

4 oz chocolate
1¼ pints milk
4 tablespoons thick grain rice
½ vanilla pod (split)
sugar (to taste)
1 egg
2 egg yolks
¼ oz butter

For caramel
4 oz granulated sugar
6 tablespoons water

Charlotte tin (1½ pints capacity)

Method
First prepare the caramel. Slowly dissolve the sugar in the water, then boil it rapidly until it is a good caramel. Stop it from further boiling by dipping bottom of pan into cold water, then pour into the tin and tilt it around gently so that the caramel coats the bottom and part of the sides. Set this aside.

Break up the chocolate, put it into a pan with the milk and simmer until it is dissolved. Then add rice and vanilla pod, simmer until the rice is tender and all the milk is absorbed (it should be of a dropping consistency). Stir rice occasionally and, if it is getting too stiff before it is cooked, add a little more milk. Draw pan aside, add sugar to taste and beat in the whole egg, egg yolks and butter. Turn this into the caramel-lined mould to fill it completely, then cover with a piece of buttered paper, and steam or cook au bain-marie for about 40-45 minutes or until it is firm to the touch. Cool rice slightly before turning out. Then pour around a little custard or chocolate sauce (see pages 101 and 146).

Crème brûlée

1 pint double cream
1 vanilla pod (split)
4 egg yolks
4-5 tablespoons caster sugar

Method
Set the oven at 325°F or Mark 3. Put the cream and vanilla pod in the top of a double boiler, cover and bring to scalding point. Meanwhile work yolks and 1 tablespoon of the sugar with a wooden spoon until light in colour.

Remove vanilla pod and pour the cream on to the egg yolks and sugar and mix well; return mixture to the pan and thicken very carefully over the heat, stirring continuously.

Watchpoint The mixture should coat the wooden spoon, but on no account allow it to boil.

Strain the mixture into a shallow ovenproof dish and place in the pre-set very moderate oven for 5-8 minutes, until a skin forms on the top. Allow cream to stand in a cool place for several hours or preferably overnight.

Pre-heat grill. Dust top of cream evenly with remaining sugar and slip it under grill at least 4 inches away from the heat. At this distance the sugar has a chance to melt before it begins to brown and an even coating of caramel over the cream is ensured. Remove the cream from under the grill and let it stand in the refrigerator for 2-3 hours before serving. A bowl of sugared fruit — raspberries, strawberries or currants, or a mixed selection — may be served separately. This makes a good contrast to the rich cream.

The crème brûlée, served here with sugared raspberries

Rice cream with pineapple

1 fresh pineapple, or 1 large can
    pineapple slices
little kirsch

For rice cream
$2\frac{1}{2}$ oz thick grain rice
$1\frac{1}{2}$ pints milk
$\frac{1}{2}$ vanilla pod
$1\frac{1}{2}$ oz caster sugar
1 egg yolk
$\frac{1}{4}$ oz gelatine
3 tablespoons pineapple juice, or
    syrup from canned pineapple,
    or water
1 carton (3-4 fl oz) double cream
    (lightly whipped)

For sugar syrup (if using fresh
    pineapple)
$\frac{1}{2}$ pint cold water
$4\frac{1}{2}$ oz granulated sugar

For decoration
glacé cherries, or crystallised
    violets and angelica, or candied
    pineapple
extra whipped cream (optional)

*Border, or ring, mould ($1\frac{1}{2}$ pints
    capacity)*

Method
Lightly oil the mould. Prepare
the rice cream. Wash the rice in
a nylon strainer under the cold
tap until the water runs clear,
then put rice in a large pan with
the milk and vanilla pod and
simmer over moderate heat until
the grains are tender and the
milk is almost absorbed, for
about 25 minutes. Remove the
vanilla pod.
Watchpoint The mixture should
look creamy at this stage — do
not let it overcook and look dry.

Add the sugar to the rice, cool
a little, then add the egg yolk.
Soak the gelatine in the pineapple juice (or syrup, or water),

Tangerine cream

then dissolve it over gentle heat; add to the rice. When the mixture is quite cold, fold in the lightly whipped cream and spoon into the mould. Leave cream in a cool place to set.

Cut away the skin of the fresh pineapple, slice and remove the core. Soak the washed peel and core in the $\frac{1}{2}$ pint of water for sugar syrup for about 30 minutes to give flavour. Strain this water on to the sugar, dissolve sugar and boil rapidly for 2 minutes, then put in the pineapple and poach for 10-15 minutes. When cool, drain the pineapple and flavour it with kirsch. If using canned pineapple drain it, do not cook in a syrup but just flavour it with kirsch.

Turn out the rice cream and arrange the pineapple slices around it. Decorate with the glacé, crystallised, or candied fruit of your choice, and cream.

3 tangerines, or clementines
6-8 sugar lumps
$\frac{3}{4}$ pint milk
1 tablespoon caster sugar
3 egg yolks
1 rounded dessertspoon gelatine
5 tablespoons cold water
1 egg white
$\frac{1}{4}$ pint double cream
2-3 tablespoons redcurrant jelly
— see page 155

Glass dessert bowl

Method

Rub the sugar lumps over the rind of the washed tangerines or clementines to remove all the zest. When well soaked with the zest, put sugar lumps in a pan with the milk and dissolve over a gentle heat. Beat yolks well with caster sugar in a bowl. Pour on the milk, return to the pan and stir over the heat until it thickens; do not let milk boil. Strain and cool.

Soften the gelatine in the water in a small pan, then heat until dissolved. Whip the egg white and then the cream. Mix the two together. Add gelatine to the custard: when beginning to thicken, fold in the cream mixture. Turn at once into a glass bowl and leave to set.

Meanwhile peel and slice the tangerines or clementines. Dissolve the redcurrant jelly over a gentle heat with about 3 tablespoons of water to make a syrup. Strain or beat it until smooth. Leave until cold. Arrange the slices of tangerine or clementines over the cream and, just before serving, coat with the syrup.

Watchpoint All custards set with gelatine should be eaten the day they are made.

1 *Adding an egg yolk to the cooked and sweetened rice after cooling*
2 *Decorating the rice cream and pineapple with crystallised violets and angelica on top of cream*

Caramel cream (Crème caramel)

1 pint milk
2 eggs
2 egg yolks
1½ tablespoons caster sugar

For caramel
4 oz lump, or granulated, sugar
½ cup water

6-inch diameter (No. 2 size) soufflé dish, or cake tin

Method

Scald milk. Break eggs into a bowl, then add the extra yolks. Beat well with a fork but do not allow to get frothy. Add sugar and milk, mix and set aside until needed.

Put sugar and water for caramel into a small pan, dissolve sugar over a gentle heat, then boil rapidly without stirring until a rich brown in colour. Stop boiling by dipping bottom of pan into a basin of cold water and, when still, pour three-quarters of caramel into a dry and warm soufflé dish or cake tin; pour rest on to an oiled plate or tin. Turn soufflé dish or cake tin carefully round to coat the caramel evenly over the bottom and sides.

Strain in the custard mixture, cover with foil or a piece of buttered paper. Cook in a bain-marie in the oven at 375°F or Mark 5 for 40-50 minutes until just set; take out and leave until cool before turning out. Crush the rest of the caramel and put round the dish.

Watchpoint A certain amount of caramel will always be left in the mould after turning out; this can be lessened by adding 1 teaspoon boiling water to caramel before pouring it into soufflé dish or cake tin. For a more creamy-textured result, use an extra egg yolk.

Coat caramel round sides of the dish, then strain in the custard

Bavarian cream (Bavarois à la crème)

3 egg yolks
2 tablespoons caster sugar
1 vanilla pod, or 2-3 drops of vanilla essence
$\frac{3}{4}$ pint milk
$\frac{1}{2}$ oz gelatine
5 tablespoons water
$\frac{1}{4}$ pint double cream

Plain mould (1 $\frac{1}{2}$ pints capacity)

Method

Cream yolks thoroughly with sugar in a bowl. Infuse pod in milk until well flavoured, or add vanilla essence to the yolk mixture. Pour milk on to the yolks, first taking out the vanilla pod. Blend well and return to the pan. Stir continually over the heat until the custard coats back of the spoon. Strain into bowl to cool.

Put the gelatine into a small pan, add the water, leave to soak for 4-5 minutes. Partially whip the cream. When the custard is cold, dissolve the gelatine over the heat. It should be quite hot before pouring into the custard. Turn into a thin pan and stand in a bowl of cold water (for quickness add a little ice to the water). Stir until beginning to thicken creamily, then add 2 tablespoons of the partially- whipped cream.

Turn custard into a lightly-oiled mould, leave to set. Then turn out carefully and spread over the rest of the cream. If wished, additional cream can be used for decorating. In this case use the whole $\frac{1}{4}$ pint for the mixture.

For a coffee bavarois : add 1 tablespoon instant coffee to the milk while bringing it to scalding point, then pour on to the yolks.

For a chocolate bavarois : break up 4 oz plain dessert chocolate and cook for 3-4 minutes in the milk.

For a good party sweet for 6-8 people, make two lots of bavarois, say a vanilla and a chocolate one. Pour the vanilla into a large plain cake tin and, when just about to set, pour in the chocolate. Gently stir round once or twice to marble the colours. Leave to set, turn out and edge with cream (or pipe a ruff of cream) round the base.

Bavarois is the name given to a rich egg custard stiffened or set with gelatine, and whipped cream added before turning into a mould. It should be velvety in consistency and must only just hold its shape when turned out.

Petits pots de crème (Small pots of cream)

A simple and delicious sweet. Cook the same way as for caramel cream (see page 94). Little, deep mousse pots made in oven-proof china should be used, otherwise ramekin pots will do. Made in a variety of flavours and arranged on a large dish these 'petits pots' look good on a buffet table. Serve plain or with cream.

The basic ingredients are $1\frac{1}{2}$ pints of milk, 3 eggs and 3 egg yolks, and 3 tablespoons caster sugar. The following flavourings may be added, adjusting the recipe where necessary:

For chocolate flavour : simmer 2 oz plain dessert chocolate in $\frac{1}{2}$ pint milk for 2-3 minutes. Then pour on to 1 egg, 1 egg yolk and 1 tablespoon of caster sugar which have been beaten together. Blend, strain and pour into pots.

For coffee flavour : dissolve 2 teaspoons instant coffee in $\frac{1}{2}$ pint hot milk; make custard as for chocolate flavour.

For vanilla flavour : infuse the milk with a vanilla pod and use vanilla sugar in place of caster sugar. When well flavoured, mix with the beaten eggs and continue to make as for the chocolate flavour.

When the pots are full, set them in water in a bain-marie or in a deep ovenproof dish on a baking sheet, covered with buttered paper; cook in oven at 350-375°F or Mark 4-5 for 12-15 minutes until just set. Take out and chill.

Caramel and vanilla bavarois

For caramel custard mixture
4 oz lump, or granulated, sugar
$\frac{1}{4}$ pint water
$\frac{1}{2}$ pint milk
3 egg yolks
1$\frac{1}{2}$ oz caster sugar
$\frac{1}{2}$ oz gelatine
5 tablespoons water

For vanilla custard mixture
1 vanilla pod, or 2-3 drops of
   vanilla essence
$\frac{3}{4}$ pint milk
3 egg yolks
1$\frac{1}{2}$ oz caster sugar
$\frac{1}{2}$ oz gelatine
5 tablespoons water
$\frac{1}{4}$ pint double cream

For sauce and decoration
6 oz lump, or granulated, sugar
$\frac{3}{4}$ cup water
$\frac{1}{4}$ pint double cream

*8-inch diameter angel cake tin;
baking tin or enamel plate, for
caramel decoration*

An angel cake tin is a round tin with
a hollow centre which is particularly effective for this dish,
but an ordinary deep, round
mould can be used.

Quantities given here will
make 1$\frac{1}{2}$ pints — enough for 6.

Method

To prepare caramel custard:
put half the $\frac{1}{4}$ pint of water in a
saucepan, dissolve lump or
granulated sugar slowly in it and
boil steadily until a rich brown
caramel. Pour on remaining
water and stir until caramel is
dissolved; stir in milk.
Watchpoint For protection when
adding the water, cover the hand
holding the pan with a cloth or
glove because the mixture will
sizzle furiously.

Cream egg yolks and caster
sugar together in a basin until
light, stir in caramel flavoured
milk, return to the saucepan and
thicken custard over a gentle
heat without letting it boil.
Watchpoint On no account must
the mixture boil or the eggs will
curdle. (Eggs cook below boiling
point.)

Strain custard into a metal
pan and cool.

Meanwhile, prepare vanilla
custard: put milk in a pan with
the vanilla pod (if using one),
bring barely to the boil and
leave to infuse. Cream egg yolks
with the sugar until light, stir in
the milk (removing vanilla pod),
and thicken in a small saucepan
over a gentle heat without
boiling. Strain and cool in a
metal pan. If using vanilla
essence, stir it in at this point.

Soak gelatine for caramel
custard in the 5 tablespoons of
water, dissolve over a gentle
heat, add to custard and set
aside.

Soak gelatine for vanilla
custard in water, dissolve over a
gentle heat, add to custard and
set aside.

Lightly whip the $\frac{1}{4}$ pint of cream
in a basin.

Set the saucepan of caramel
custard in a bowl containing
cold water and 2-3 ice cubes and
stir until the custard begins to
set. (A metal saucepan responds
to temperature changes more
quickly than a pottery bowl, so
custard sets faster if kept in
saucepan.)
Watchpoint It is important to stir
from time to time or the custard
mixture will not set smoothly.

Fold in half the whipped
cream and pour caramel custard
mixture into lightly-oiled tin.

Cool vanilla custard in the same way and fold in remainder of whipped cream as custard begins to set.

Pour the vanilla custard into the cake tin, swirling a knife through the two mixtures to give a marbled effect. (Cake tin will not be full to top.) Leave in a cool place to set.

To prepare sauce : dissolve sugar in half the water, boil steadily to a rich brown caramel and then pour a little on to the oiled tin or plate. Leave to set, and keep for decoration. Meanwhile slowly add the rest of the water to caramel remaining in the saucepan (not forgetting to cover with a cloth the hand with which you hold the pan while the mixture sizzles). Stir carefully until caramel has dissolved. Pour sauce into a basin and leave to cool.

Turn out bavarois on to a serving dish. To do this, loosen sides with a palette or table knife, easing the knife down to the bottom at one spot and letting in a little air to release the vacuum. Put the serving plate over the top of the tin and turn over. Hold plate and tin and shake once or twice from side to side, when the bavarois should side out quite easily.

Watchpoint Never dip a creamy sweet in hot water to loosen as this spoils the appearance ; it is only done for jellies which are much firmer mixtures.

For decoration : whip remaining $\frac{1}{4}$ pint of cream until firm enough to pipe. Crush sheet of caramel (from tin or enamel plate) into small pieces. Pipe rosettes of whipped cream over the bavarois and decorate with crushed caramel. Serve sauce separately.

Custard tart

For rich shortcrust pastry
6 oz flour
4 oz butter
1 rounded dessertspoon caster sugar
1 egg yolk
2 tablespoon water

For custard filling
3 eggs
1 tablespoon caster sugar
½ pint milk
2-3 drops of vanilla essence
nutmeg (grated)

*6-inch diameter flan ring, or cake tin,
or deep small moulds*

Traditionally an English dish, it can be made in a deep flan ring or tin, or in small deep moulds so that a good proportion of custard goes with the pastry.

> **Vanilla pods** give a particularly delicate flavour to custard or cream. These pods can be bought separately and used several times over. Little white crystals on the pod indicate its freshness.
>
> The seeds hold most of the flavour, so it is best to split pod and scrape out some of the tiny black seeds to use with it. Once used rinse pod in warm water, allow to dry before putting away in a small jar of caster sugar. Keep well stoppered; this vanilla sugar may be used instead of vanilla essence for flavouring cakes and custards.

Method

First prepare pastry (see method, page 12) and set aside to chill. Then roll out and line into the flan ring (or small moulds) and set on a baking sheet. Prick the bottoms very lightly, then put baking sheet into the refrigerator while the custard is made.

Break eggs into a bowl, mix with a fork, add sugar, milk and vanilla essence. Strain mixture, then pour into the flan ring. Fill to about $\frac{1}{4}$ inch below the top. Grate a little nutmeg over top.

Set the oven at 400°F or Mark 6, and put a second baking sheet on the top shelf to heat. When thoroughly hot set first baking sheet (from refrigerator) with the flan ring or moulds on top of the second one which will heat it up quickly; this helps to cook bottom of pastry. Bake for about 15-20 minutes, or until the custard is set. After 7 minutes reduce the heat to 350°F or Mark 4. When set, take custard out and cool. Lift the flan ring off carefully or turn custard tarts out of the moulds. Serve cold.

Custard pudding

1 pint milk
strip of lemon rind (optional)
2 eggs
2 egg yolks
$1\frac{1}{2}$ tablespoons caster sugar
2-3 drops vanilla essence
    (optional)
butter
nutmeg (grated) — optional

7-inch diameter pie dish

Method
Butter the pie dish. Scald the milk by heating to just under boiling point (with the lemon rind). Beat the eggs and yolks together until well mixed but not frothy. Add the sugar (and the vanilla). Pour on the milk, blend, take out the lemon rind if being used and strain custard into the pie dish. Dot the surface with a little butter and grate over a little nutmeg.

Stand the dish in a bain-marie and cook in the oven for 35-40 minutes at 350-375°F or Mark 4-5. The pudding should be just set and have a nice brown top. Serve hot or cold.

Custard sauce

(Crème à la vanille)

$\frac{1}{2}$ pint creamy milk
2 tablespoons caster sugar
2-3 drops of vanilla essence, or
    $\frac{1}{2}$ vanilla pod (split)
2 egg yolks

Method
Put the milk in a pan, add the sugar with vanilla essence or, if using a vanilla pod, infuse it in milk for 10 minutes, keeping pan covered. Take out pod, then add sugar.

Cream the yolks in a bowl, bring the milk to scalding point and pour on gradually. Blend mixture together and return to the pan; stir continually over a gentle heat with a wooden spatula or spoon. Stir gently to avoid splashing. When the custard coats the spoon and looks creamy, strain back into the bowl.

Dredge a little caster sugar over the top and leave to cool. This coating of sugar melts and helps prevent a skin forming.

Watchpoint Should the custard get too hot and begin to curdle, turn at once into the basin without straining and whisk briskly for 2-3 seconds. Remember that gentle heat helps to prevent a custard from curdling and makes it creamier.

Chocolate cream

12 oz plain chocolate
$\frac{1}{4}$ pint strong coffee
$\frac{3}{4}$ pint creamy milk
3 tablespoons cornflour
caster sugar (to taste)
2 tablespoons brandy (optional)
1 small carton (2$\frac{1}{2}$ fl oz) double
   cream

Plain mould (1 pint capacity)

Method
Break up the chocolate and dissolve in the coffee. When this reaches boiling point, add $\frac{1}{2}$ pint of the milk, stir well until it reboils and then draw pan aside.

Mix cornflour with rest of the milk, add it to the pan and cook gently, stirring well for 3-4 minutes. Sweeten to taste, draw pan aside and add the brandy; allow the cream to cool, stirring it occasionally. Whip cream lightly, then fold it into the mixture. Turn cream at once into the wet mould and leave to set; turn out when cold.

Peruvian cream

scant 1$\frac{1}{4}$ pints milk
2$\frac{1}{4}$ oz coffee beans
1-2 drops of vanilla essence
3$\frac{1}{2}$ oz caster sugar
2 tablespoons hot water
3$\frac{1}{2}$ oz chocolate
5 egg yolks
1 whole egg

6-inch diameter top (No. 2 size) soufflé dish, or shallow pie dish (1$\frac{1}{2}$ pints capacity)

Method
Infuse the milk with the coffee beans; when well flavoured, strain it and add the vanilla essence. Cook the caster sugar to a light caramel in a small pan; stop it further cooking by touching the base of the pan in cold water. Add the hot water to caramel and dissolve over gentle heat. Keep this on one side.

Break up the chocolate, place it in a pan with a little of the coffee-flavoured milk and dissolve it over very gentle heat. Work it until chocolate is smooth, then add to the remaining milk with the caramel. Beat yolks and egg, pour on the liquid, then turn cream into the dish; cook gently au bain-marie for about 25 minutes until set. Remove dish and leave to cool.

To serve, leave cream plain or cover with lightly whipped cream and decorate with chocolate caraque (see page 59).

Gâteaux and pastries

Europe provides a rich store of delicious gâteaux, the most famous of which are perhaps from Vienna, with France not far behind. To make these gâteaux is really a specialist's job and indeed few people abroad would dream of doing so, buying instead from their local pâtisserie. Although continental pâtisseries flourish in some of our big cities, they are a rarity, so it can be an adventure to try making these gâteaux yourself.

Remember that care and attention to detail is vitally important and that scales must be used to measure ingredients. In some of the recipes in this section, we have given the gram equivalent of weights; this ensures greater accuracy than is possible to achieve with the avoirdupois system. Indeed, if this type of gâteau is to be made fairly frequently, it is a good idea to invest in a set of French weights, or to use scales which give both measuring systems.

A special pastry called French flan pastry (pâté sucrée, or sèche) is largely used for pâtis-series and certain gâteaux, as well as for flans and tartlets, because it stands up better than shortcrust to being filled with fruit and glazed. French flan pastry is best made at least an hour before rolling out and baking, or it can be made up and stored in a polythene bag in the refrigerator, where it will keep satisfactorily for two or three days. Once filled, these gâteaux are best eaten the same day.

Puff pastry is also often used for gâteaux. Once made, this can be rolled out, cut to shape and stored, wrapped in grease-proof paper and a cloth. It will keep for 24-48 hours in a cool place.

When fresh summer fruits are not available, chocolate is a popular choice for decorating gâteaux and pastries. When cooking with chocolate, choose a good quality plain block chocolate that is not too sweet. This will give a good flavour and will melt readily, when warmed on a plate, for use as caraque or where a thin coating of chocolate is called for.

Professional pâtissiers use a

special chocolate known as 'couverture'. In some recipes, unsweetened chocolate is mentioned. This gives a specially good flavour and rich colour, but is not always easy to obtain. As a substitute, a mixture of sweet chocolate and cocoa can be used. When using cocoa as a substitute for chocolate in cake-making, always cook it with a little water to a cream. Boil it gently until it will drop easily from the spoon and keep it well stirred.

For coating cakes, first melt the chocolate without water. Cut it into small pieces, or grate it onto a plate and set this over a pan of warm water. When the chocolate starts to melt, work well with a palette, or round-bladed, knife. This helps to keep the chocolate glossy when set. It is important not to allow it to get more than lukewarm (just over blood heat, 98°F), or it will be dull in appearance when cold; allow it to cool at room temperature (don't put it in a refrigerator as this will also dull the gloss).

These gâteaux and pastries are ideal as party puddings. They can usually be made in advance, so that a dinner party host or hostess is left free at the last minute to attend to a hot main course. For buffet parties they have the added advantage that guests can easily manage them using only a fork, and can even cope standing up, if necessary. Many of the recipes we have included will serve 6-8 people.

Gâteau au chocolat

3 oz plain flour
pinch of salt
8 oz plain block chocolate
8 oz butter
8 oz caster sugar
7 eggs (separated)
4 oz ground almonds (see page 155)
1 teaspoon sal volatile
1 lb white fondant icing(see page 110)
1 teaspoon rum

8-inch diameter cake tin

Method
Prepare the tin by lining it with buttered greaseproof paper. Set oven at 350°F or Mark 4.

Sift the flour with the salt. Cut up the chocolate and place it on a plate over a pan of warm water to melt. Cream the butter, add the sugar and beat until it is soft and white. Beat in the egg yolks one at a time, the melted chocolate and the almonds. Whisk the egg whites until stiff and fold them into the mixture with the sal volatile and sifted flour.

Turn mixture into the prepared tin and bake in pre-set slow oven for about 50-60 minutes, reducing the heat to 325°F or Mark 3 after the first 30 minutes. When the cake is cool, ice with rum-flavoured fondant icing (see page 110).

Royal icing

1 lb icing sugar
2 egg whites

Method
Whisk egg whites until frothy. Add icing sugar 1 tablespoon at a time, beating thoroughly between each addition. Continue beating until mixture will stand in peaks. Flavour if wished.

Gâteau mexicain

3 oz plain flour
pinch of salt
2 oz butter
1½ oz cocoa
1 teacup water
4 eggs
4½ oz caster sugar
chocolate butter cream (see page 56)
apricot jam glaze (see page 11)
chocolate fondant icing (see page 110)
royal icing — opposite

Deep 9½-inch diameter cake tin

Method
Set oven at 350°F or Mark 4, grease the tin. Sift the flour with the salt, warm the butter until it is soft but not oily, and pours easily. Mix the cocoa with the water in a small pan, cook it gently to a thick cream, then set it aside to cool.

Whisk eggs, add sugar gradually and then whisk over a pan of hot water until thick and mousse-like. Remove pan from the heat and continue whisking until the bowl is cold; stir in the prepared cocoa. Fold two-thirds of the flour into the cocoa mixture, then the melted butter and lastly the remaining flour.

Watchpoint This mixing of the flour and butter must be done lightly and quickly, using a metal spoon.

Turn the cake mixture into the tin and bake in pre-set very moderate oven for about 40 minutes. When cool, cut cake in two and sandwich with chocolate butter cream. Reshape and brush all over with a thin layer of apricot jam glaze. Ice the gâteau and, before icing sets, marble it with a little white royal icing.

105

Gâteau basque

For rich shortcrust pastry
6 oz plain flour
pinch of salt
1 oz shortening
3 oz butter
3 rounded dessertspoons ground
  almonds
6 dessertspoons caster sugar
1 egg yolk
2-3 drops of vanilla essence
2-3 tablespoons cold water
4-5 heaped tablespoons jam
  (preferably plum, gooseberry,
  damson, etc.)
1 egg white (lightly beaten)
caster sugar (for dusting)

6-7 inch diameter flan ring

Method
Prepare the pastry (see method, page 12).

Roll out two-thirds of the dough to $\frac{1}{4}$ - $\frac{1}{2}$ inch thickness and line on to the flan ring. Fill with the jam, roll out the rest of the dough to a round and lay over the top. Press down the edges, mark the surface, cart-wheel-fashion, with the point of a knife. Bake for 30-35 minutes in an oven at 400°F or Mark 6. Lower oven temperature to 375°F or Mark 5 after the first 15 minutes.

Just before the gâteau is ready, brush the top with a little lightly beaten egg white, dust immediately with caster sugar and return to the oven for about 2 minutes to frost the top. Serve hot or cold.

Watchpoint The sugar must be dusted on to the egg white quickly, before the heat of the pastry has a chance to set the egg white, so that the sugar and egg white combine to make a meringue-like topping of frost.

Gâteau moka aux amandes

3 oz plain flour
pinch of salt
3 eggs
$4\frac{1}{2}$ oz caster sugar

To finish
butter cream (see page 56)
coffee essence (to flavour)
3 oz almonds (blanched, split and
  shredded) — see page 13
icing sugar

$9\frac{1}{2}$-inch diameter layer cake tin

This gives about 10 portions. The cake can be made and decorated the day before ; store it in an airtight tin.

Method
Set the oven at 370°F or Mark 4-5. Prepare the tin.

Sift the flour with salt. Break the eggs into a bowl, add the sugar gradually and then whisk over a pan of hot water until the mixture is thick and white (and forms a ribbon trail). Remove bowl from the heat and continue beating until the bowl is cold. Fold the flour into the mixture, using a tablespoon. Pour the mixture at once into the tin and bake it in pre-set oven for 25-30 minutes. Turn the cake on to a wire rack to cool.

Have ready the butter cream well flavoured with the coffee essence. Bake almonds to a light golden-brown.

Split the cake and sandwich with a thin layer of the coffee butter cream. Reshape and spread the top and sides with more of the same cream, press the browned almonds all over the cake, dredge lightly with icing sugar and then decorate round the top edge with rosettes of butter cream.

Austrian coffee cake

6 oz butter
6 oz caster sugar
3 eggs
6 oz self-raising flour
pinch of salt
½ pint strong black coffee
sugar and rum, or brandy, (to taste)
½ pint cream (whipped)
1-2 drops of vanilla essence
almonds (browned)

*Ring mould (1½ pints capacity, or
8-inch diameter cake tin*

*Austrian coffee cake is one of the
more decorative sweets. The cake
is soaked in sweetened coffee that
has been flavoured with rum or
brandy; it is then covered with
whipped cream and almonds*

Method
Set the oven at 375°F or Mark 5.
Cream the butter in a bowl, add
the sugar and cream again until
light and fluffy. Beat in the eggs
a little at a time and lastly fold
in the sifted flour and salt with
a metal spoon. Turn the mixture
into the prepared mould and
bake for about 25 minutes. (If
using cake tin, bake for 35-40
minutes.)

When cooked, take cake out
of oven and set aside to cool.
When cold, soak it with the
coffee, sweetened, and flavoured
with rum or brandy; mask (coat)
with the cream, sweetened, and
flavoured with vanilla essence.
Decorate with the browned
almonds.

Chestnut and chocolate cake

$\frac{3}{4}$ lb chestnuts
3 oz plain dessert chocolate
4 tablespoons water
4 large eggs
8 oz caster sugar

For filling
3 oz plain dessert chocolate
3 tablespoons water
2 egg yolks
$\frac{1}{2}$ pint (or slightly less) double cream
caster sugar and rum (to taste)

Two 9-inch diameter sandwich tins

Method
Grease sandwich tins and line the bases with non-stick (silicone) cooking paper. Set the oven at 350°F or Mark 4. Skin, cook and sieve the chestnuts and check the weight (see page 51). You need 8 oz for the cake.

Melt the first 3 oz of chocolate in 4 tablespoons water over very gentle heat to a thick cream and leave to cool. Separate the eggs, beat the yolks with the sugar until thick and white, then add the chocolate. Whisk the egg whites until stiff and dry and fold into the mixture with the chestnuts. Pour half the mixture into each tin and bake 35-40 minutes. Turn out carefully and leave to cool.

To prepare the filling: melt the remaining chocolate in the water and bring just to the boil. Beat in the egg yolks, one at a time, and leave to cool. Whip the cream until thick, then fold into the chocolate with sugar and rum to taste. It looks good if the mixture is left rather streaky. Sandwich the cakes together with the chocolate cream, reserving some to spread on top.

Doboz torte

5 oz (150 g) plain flour
pinch of salt
4 eggs
6 oz (180 g) caster sugar
8 oz quantity butter cream
(flavoured with 4 oz (120 g)
plain chocolate) — see page 56

For caramel
5 oz (150 g) lump sugar
$\frac{1}{4}$ pint water

To finish
crushed caramel (optional)
grated chocolate (optional)
chocolate butter cream (for
rosettes)

This cake is of Austrian origin.

Method
Prepare 6 baking sheets by brushing them with melted lard or oil and dusting lightly with flour; then mark an 8-inch circle on each one, using a plate or pan lid as a guide. Set the oven at 375°F or Mark 5.

Sift the flour with the salt. Break the eggs in a bowl, add the sugar. Place bowl over pan of hot water on gentle heat and whisk mixture until it is thick and white. Remove bowl from the heat and continue whisking until it is cold. Lightly fold the flour into the mixture, using a metal spoon. Divide mixture into 6 portions and spread each over a circle on the prepared sheets (this can be done using fewer sheets in rotation, but each time the baking sheet to be re-used must be wiped, re-greased and floured). Bake in a pre-set moderate oven for about 5-6 minutes.

Trim each round with a sharp knife while still on the baking sheet, then lift on to a wire rack to cool. Take 1 round, lay it on an oiled sheet ready to coat with the caramel.

To prepare caramel: melt the sugar in the water over a very low heat without boiling. When completely dissolved, increase the heat and cook it rapidly to a rich brown caramel. Pour this at once over the single cake round and, when caramel is just about set, mark it into portions with an oiled knife and trim edges.

Sandwich the six rounds together with chocolate butter cream, putting the caramel-covered round on top. Spread the sides with more butter cream and press round crushed caramel or grated chocolate. Pipe a rosette of butter cream on each portion.

Doboz torte is decorated with crushed caramel and chocolate-flavoured butter cream rosettes

Gâteau Mercédès

8 oz quantity of French flan
pastry

For almond filling
8½ oz (250 g) ground almonds
8½ oz (250 g) caster sugar
4 egg whites
kirsch (to flavour)
2½ oz (75 g) crystallised fruits
3 tablespoons apricot jam
1½-2 oz shredded almonds
apricot glaze (see page 11)

8-inch diameter spring-form tin

Method
Make French flan pastry (see
method, page 14, adjusting
quantities). Chill for 30 minutes.
   Set oven at 350°F or Mark 4.
   To prepare filling: pound the
almonds and sugar with the egg
whites and flavour with kirsch.
Shred the fruits and moisten
them with the jam.
   Roll out the chilled pastry and
line it into the tin; prick the
base of the pastry lightly with
a fork and place the fruits on it.
Fill the flan with the almond
mixture and cover this with the
shredded almonds. Bake in a
very moderate pre-set oven for
about 45 minutes until set and
golden-brown. When gâteau is
cool, brush with apricot glaze.

*Pouring the almond mixture on top
of the fruit in the pastry case*

Fondant icing

1 lump sugar
8 tablespoons water
pinch of cream of tartar

A sugar thermometer is essential
for this recipe.
   You can now buy blocks or
packets of powder of fondant
icing. Simply follow the manufacturer's instructions.

Method
Place the sugar and water in a
saucepan and dissolve without
stirring over a low heat. Using
a brush dipped in cold water,
wipe round pan at level of the
syrup to prevent a crust forming.
Add the cream of tartar (dissolved in 1 teaspoon of water),
place the lid on the pan,
increase the heat and bring to
the boil.
   Remove the lid after 2 minutes,
put a sugar thermometer in and
boil the syrup steadily to 240°F.
When it has reached this
temperature take the pan off the
heat at once, wait for the
bubbles to subside then pour
the mixture very slowly on to
a damp marble or laminated
plastic slab. Work with a
wooden spatula until it becomes a firm and white fondant.
Take a small piece of fondant at
a time and knead with the
fingertips until smooth.
   For storing, pack fondant
icing in an airtight jar or tin.
When you want to use it, gently
warm the fondant with a little
sugar syrup to make a smooth
cream. The icing should then
flow easily. Flavour and colour
it just before use with vanilla,
lemon, etc. Spread over cake
with a palette knife.

Nusskuchen

4 oz butter
4 oz caster sugar
2 eggs
1½ oz ground hazelnuts (toasted)
1 teaspoon instant coffee
1 tablespoon warm milk
4 oz self-raising flour
pinch of salt

For filling
1 lb dessert apples (Cox's orange
pippin variety) — peeled, cored
and sliced
2 tablespoons apricot jam
grated rind and juice of ½ lemon

To decorate
icing sugar (for dusting), or 2 oz
plain chocolate (melted)

8-inch diameter sandwich tin

Method

Grease and flour the tin; set oven at 375°F or Mark 5.

Soften the butter in a bowl, add the sugar and work until light and fluffy. Separate the eggs and beat the yolks into the butter and sugar. Stir in the prepared nuts. Dissolve the coffee in the warm milk; sift the flour with the salt and whisk the egg whites until stiff.

Fold the flour into the mixture with the coffee-flavoured milk, then fold in the egg whites. Turn mixture into the prepared tin and bake in pre-set oven for about 25 minutes until cake is firm to the touch and has shrunk slightly from the sides of the tin. Turn on to a rack to cool.

Meanwhile peel, core and slice the apples and place in a shallow pan with the jam, lemon rind and juice. Cover and cook until apples are soft; leave to cool.

Split the cake in half and fill with the cooled apple mixture. Finish with a dusting of icing sugar or spread with the melted chocolate, using a palette knife.

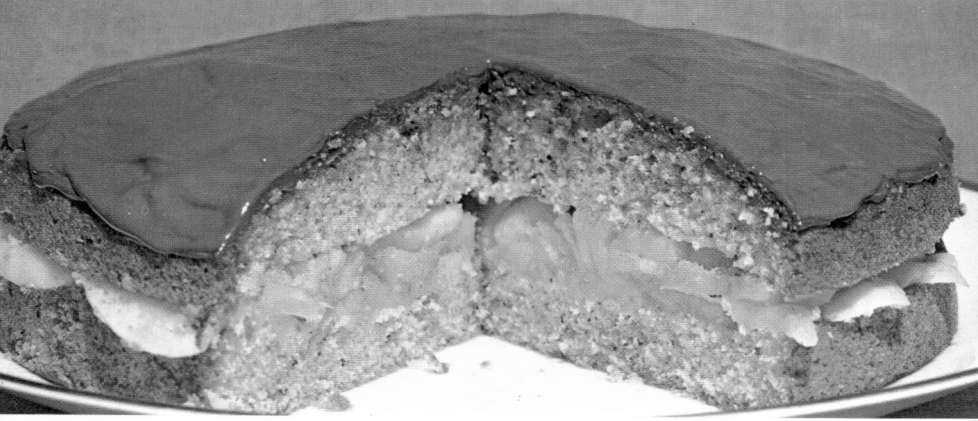

Russian tipsy cake

1 oz unsweetened chocolate
3 tablespoons water
3 eggs
4½ oz caster sugar
2¼ oz flour (very well sifted with
a pinch of salt)
1 tablespoon flour
2-3 tablespoons sugar syrup (see
page 39) — flavoured with 2-3
tablespoons brandy, or rum
½ pint double cream
a few drops of vanilla essence
2 oz block chocolate (for making
caraque — see page 59)

8-9 inch diameter sandwich tin

Method

Prepare the tin (grease with some melted shortening, then dust with caster sugar and with sifted flour) and set the oven at 375°F or Mark 5. Melt the chocolate in the water until it forms a thick cream, then leave it to cool.

To make the sponge cake: whisk the eggs and sugar together in a bowl over a pan of hot water (or use an electric mixer at high speed, without heat) until thick and mousselike. Remove from the heat and whisk until mixture is cold. Fold in the flour. Divide the mixture in two and add the prepared chocolate to one portion and the extra tablespoon of flour to the other.

Put the two mixtures into the prepared tin, alternating spoonfuls of light and dark. Draw a knife through to give a marbled effect and bake in the pre-set oven for 40-50 minutes or until the cake feels done (it must spring back immediately when pressed with the finger).

When the cake is cool, split it and spoon a little of the flavoured syrup over both halves. Whip and sweeten the cream and flavour it with vanilla essence. Fill the cake with cream, reserving some for decoration. Reshape the cake and moisten it with any remaining syrup. Decorate the cake with chocolate caraque and rosettes of cream.

Decorating the tipsy cake with scrolls of chocolate caraque, after filling and decorating it with the whipped double cream

Hedgehog tipsy cake

1 sponge, or madeira, cake
2 wineglasses sweet white wine
1 glass sweet sherry
1 wineglass fruit syrup (from stewed, or canned, fruit)
2 oz almonds (blanched and shredded)
apricot glaze (see page 11)

For syllabub
2 large oranges
1 lemon
2-3 oz caster sugar
½ pint double cream

7½-inch oval fluted jelly mould (for home-made cake)

Ingredients above are solely for this size jelly mould.

Method
The cake can be bought or home-made, but must be stale. If home-made, make cake in an oval jelly mould. Trim to resemble shape of a hedgehog's back and hollow out top with a round cutter, reserving the cut-out piece. Then set the cake on a serving dish.

Mix wines and syrup together in a bowl and pour into hollow in cake. As liquids run through, baste the cake well so that it is thoroughly soaked. Put back cut-out piece of cake and baste again. Leave overnight.

To blanch and shred almonds : pour boiling water over the shelled nuts, cover and leave to cool. Drain, rinse in cold water, and press off skins with your fingers. Rinse and dry thoroughly. Split in two and cut each half lengthways into fine pieces.

Spread shredded almonds on a baking sheet and bake to a golden-brown in oven at 350°F or Mark 4. Heat apricot glaze and brush over cake. Stick almonds into cake on top and sides, sloping all one way to resemble quills. Start at the back and continue all the way up to the 'nose'.

To make syllabub : squeeze juice from oranges and lemon separately and measure. There should be one-quarter the quantity of lemon to orange. Dissolve sugar in mixed juices in a pan over low heat, remove from heat and allow to cool. Whisk cream and when thickening, pour in liquid. Continue whisking until thick, then spoon round hedgehog cake.

Apple and hazelnut galette

3 oz hazelnuts (shelled)
3 oz butter
2 rounded tablespoons caster
  sugar
4½ oz plain flour
pinch of salt

For filling
1 lb dessert apples (pippin variety)
1 tablespoon smooth apricot jam
grated rind of 1 lemon
1 tablespoon orange peel (finely
  chopped)
2 tablespoons sultanas
2 tablespoons currants
icing sugar (for dusting)
whipped cream (optional)

A **galette** is a round flat cake,
usually made of flaky pastry.

*Rosettes of whipped cream piped
on to each portion of the apple and
hazelnut galette make an elegant
decoration. Finish off with a hazelnut in the centre of each rosette*

Method
Brown the shelled nuts in the
oven at 350°F or Mark 4 until
husks can be rubbed off (about
7-8 minutes, when nuts should
be a deep golden-brown). Reserve a few whole nuts for decoration and pass remainder
through a small cheese grater
or mincer, or work until fine in
a blender.

Soften the butter, add sugar
and beat together until light and
fluffy. Sift the flour with a pinch
of salt and stir into the mixture
with the prepared nuts. Chill for
at least 30 minutes.

Meanwhile prepare filling.
Peel, core and slice the apples.
Put them in a pan with apricot
jam and grated lemon rind. Cook
over slow heat until soft, then
add orange peel, sultanas and
currants; simmer for another 5
minutes.

Divide the pastry mixture in
two and place each piece on a
lightly-floured baking sheet. Roll
or pat into very thin rounds 9
inches in diameter. Bake for
about 10 minutes in the oven at
375°F or Mark 5.
Watchpoint Do not let pastry
brown or it will taste scorched.
While still warm and on the
baking sheet, trim edges and cut
one round into eight portions,
then slide carefully on to a wire
rack to cool.

Cover the whole round of
pastry with apple mixture, spread
evenly and place the cut portions
on top. Dust with icing sugar.
Serve with whipped cream, or
pipe rosettes of cream on each
portion and decorate with whole
hazelnuts.

Basic puff pastry

8 oz plain flour
pinch of salt
8 oz butter
1 teaspoon lemon juice
scant $\frac{1}{4}$ pint water (ice cold)

To have perfect results when making puff pastry, you must use the right kind of flour and fat, and always use ice-cold water for mixing.

It is also important to work in a very cool atmosphere. Never attempt to make puff pastry in very hot weather; it will become sticky and difficult to handle. Make it early in the morning (if possible before you have done any cooking), as a kitchen soon becomes warm and steamy.

Fat should be cool and firm. The best puff pastry for flavour and texture is made from butter; this should be of a firm consistency and slightly salted — such as English, Australian or New Zealand. Continental butters are too creamy in texture and result in a sticky pastry, difficult to handle. If margarine has to be used, again use a firm variety (one that does not spread easily). The cheapest varieties of butter and margarine are the best for this purpose.

Flour should be 'strong', ie. a bread flour which has a high gluten content. It should also be well sifted and quite cool.

Method

Sift flour and salt into a bowl. Rub in a piece of butter the size of a walnut. Add lemon juice to water, make a well in centre of flour and pour in about two-thirds of the liquid. Mix with a palette, or round-bladed, knife. When the dough is beginning to form, add remaining water.

Turn out the dough on to a marble slab, a laminated-plastic work top, or a board, dusted with flour. Knead dough for 2-3 minutes, then roll out to a square about $\frac{1}{2}$-$\frac{3}{4}$ inch thick.

Beat butter, if necessary, to make it pliable and place in centre of dough. Fold this up over butter to enclose it completely (sides and ends over centre like a parcel). Wrap in a cloth or piece of greaseproof paper and put in the refrigerator for 10-15 minutes.

Flour slab or work top, put on dough, the join facing upwards, and bring rolling pin down on to dough 3-4 times to flatten it slightly.

Now roll out to a rectangle about $\frac{1}{2}$ - $\frac{3}{4}$ inch thick. Fold into three, ends to middle, as accurately as possible, if necessary pulling the ends to keep them rectangular. Seal the edges with your hand or rolling pin and turn pastry half round to bring the edge towards you. Roll out again and fold in three (keep a note of the 'turns' given). Set pastry aside in refrigerator for 15 minutes.

Repeat this process, giving a total of 6 turns with three 15-minute rests after each two turns. Then leave in the refrigerator until wanted.

Gâteau mille feuilles au citron

1½ lb quantity of puff pastry
   (see page 115)
2¼ pints double cream
1 lb apricot glaze (see page 11)

For lemon curd filling
8 oz caster sugar
4 oz unsalted butter
grated rind and juice of 2 large
   lemons
3 eggs (well beaten)

For decoration
small shapes made from
   trimmings of puff pastry
crystallised fruits
almonds, or pistachio nuts

4-5 inch diameter plain cutter

Method

Set oven at 400°F or Mark 6, and dampen a baking sheet.

Roll out pastry very thinly and cut 6 rounds the size of a dessert plate; remove the centres of each round with the cutter to leave a large ring of pastry. From remaining pastry cut 3 plain circles, a little thicker and larger than the rings, to form bases for each cake.

Place the pastry rings on the baking sheet, prick them well with a fork and bake in pre-set hot oven for 8 minutes. Then prick and bake the circles on a dampened baking sheet for 12-15 minutes. Make any pastry trimmings into tiny stars, diamonds, etc., bake in the hot oven for 5-7 minutes, or until brown, then leave to cool.

Put all the ingredients for lemon curd into an enamel pan or stone jam jar standing in boiling water. Stir gently over low heat until mixture is thick. (It must not boil or it will curdle.) Pour into a bowl and allow to cool.

When all the pastry is cool, brush with warm apricot glaze and mount one ring on top of another on a base. Each gâteau has one plain circle as a base and two rings. Brush the top and sides of each gâteau with apricot glaze and decorate with the small pastry shapes, crystallised fruit or chopped nuts.

To serve : reserve a little cream for decoration and whip the remainder until it begins to thicken, then fold in the lemon curd. Divide between the gâteaux and decorate the top with rosettes of whipped cream, crystallised fruit and chopped nuts.

Top : decorating gâteau mille feuilles with small pastry shapes and crystallised fruit
Above : decorating the gâteau with rosettes of whipped cream

116

Apricot and almond strudel

¾ lb fresh ripe apricots
3 oz granulated, or caster, sugar

For almond filling
3 oz ground almonds
2 oz caster sugar
½ egg (lightly beaten)
2 tablespoons double cream

For strudel paste
8 oz plain flour
pinch of salt
1 small egg
1 dessertspoon salad oil
4 fl oz warm water

melted butter
icing sugar (for dusting)

Method
Split and stone the apricots. Slice each half into a bowl with 3 oz sugar. Combine the ground almonds, 2 oz caster sugar, egg and cream and mix to a smooth paste.

Make the strudel paste by sifting the flour with a pinch of salt into a warm bowl. Make a well in the centre and pour in the lightly beaten egg and the oil, mixed with about 4 fl oz of warm water. Beat well until the paste is thoroughly elastic. It should be really soft, but if it is too slack, add a little flour. When well beaten turn into a clean bowl, dust lightly with flour, cover with a plate and leave in a warm place for about 7-10 minutes.

Lay a large tea towel on the table and flour it lightly. Flatten the paste by rolling slightly, then lay it on the floured cloth. Leave for a further 5 minutes before starting to pull gently from the sides. When paper thin dab the top liberally with melted butter. Scatter over the apricots, then divide the almond filling over the top. Tilt the cloth to roll up the strudel, then tip it on to a well greased baking sheet, curling it slightly. Brush again with melted butter then bake in a hot oven, 400°F or Mark 6, for 15-20 minutes or until nicely brown and crisp. Take out and dust well with icing sugar. Serve, preferably just warm, with a bowl of lightly whipped cream.

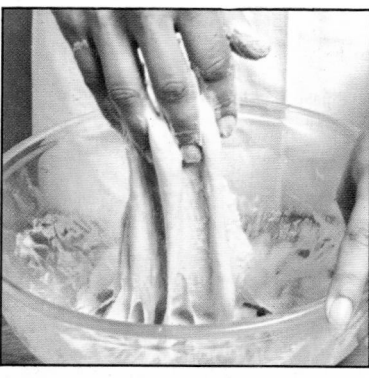

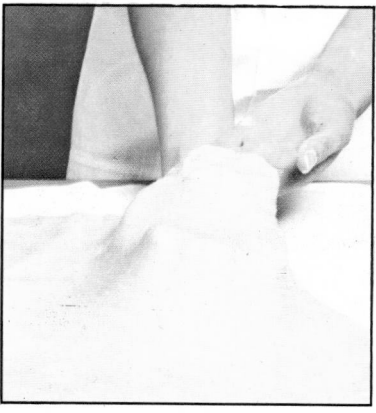

Above left : beating strudel by hand until it is soft and elastic
Left : putting the dough out on a tea towel until it is paper-thin

Chocolate mille feuilles

6 oz quantity of puff pastry
   (see page 115)
12 oz chestnuts
2 tablespoons milk
7½-10 fl oz double cream
vanilla sugar, or few drops of
   vanilla essence
little caster sugar

For topping
4 oz plain chocolate
2-3 tablespoons strong black
   coffee, or water
few drops of oil

Method

Set the oven at 425°F or Mark 7. Have the pastry well chilled; roll out to a large sheet about 12 inches by 9 inches, lay on a dampened baking sheet and prick well. Chill for about 10 minutes before putting it into the pre-set oven. Bake for 20-25 minutes or until a good brown. Take out of the oven and, using two palette knives or a slice, turn the pastry over. Replace in the oven and bake until well browned and crisp. Take out and allow to get quite cold.

Meanwhile skin the chestnuts and simmer them in enough water to cover, with the milk, for 20-30 minutes or until tender, then drain and rub through a wire sieve on to a flat dish.

Scattering half of the chestnut purée over the cream-covered pastry, to make chocolate mille feuilles

Spreading chocolate and coffee mixture over the top layer of pastry (finished mille feuilles is right)

Leave until quite cold. The chestnut purée should be very dry and powdery. Whip the cream lightly, flavour with vanilla and sweeten to taste.

Trim the edges of the pastry and cut into three even lengths. Spread one of these thickly with half the cream and scatter over half the chestnut purée. Press second piece of pastry lightly on top of this and repeat the cream and chestnut layers. Press the third piece of pastry lightly down on top.

Melt the chocolate with the coffee (or water), being careful not to get it warmer than blood heat (it should be the consistency of thick cream) and add the oil. Spread the melted chocolate over the top of the pastry. Crush the pastry trimmings and sprinkle them around the edge.

Basic choux pastry

Quantity for 3-4 people
$\frac{1}{4}$ pint (5 fl oz) water
2 oz butter, or margarine
$2\frac{1}{2}$ oz plain flour
2 eggs

Quantity for 4-6 people
$7\frac{1}{2}$ fl oz water
3 oz butter, or margarine
$3\frac{3}{4}$ oz plain flour
3 eggs

Method
Put water and fat into a fairly large pan. Sift flour on to a piece of paper. Bring contents of the pan to the boil and when bubbling draw pan aside, allow bubbles to subside and pour in all the flour at once. Stir vigorously until it is smooth (a few seconds).

Cool mixture for about 5 minutes, then beat in the eggs one at a time. If eggs are large, break the last one into a bowl and beat with a fork. Add this slowly to ensure that the mixture remains firm and keeps its shape (you may not need to use all of this last egg).

Beat pastry for about 3 minutes until it looks glossy.

Choux pastry should be baked in a hot oven on a rising temperature, ie. baked for 10 minutes at 400°F or Mark 6, then the cooking completed at 425°F or Mark 7 for the length of time given in the recipe.

Pastry cream

1 egg (separated)
1 egg yolk
2 oz caster sugar
$\frac{3}{4}$ oz plain flour
$\frac{1}{2}$ oz cornflour
$\frac{1}{2}$ pint milk
2-3 oz plain chocolate, or 1-$1\frac{1}{2}$ tablespoons coffee essence (optional)

Method
To make $\frac{1}{2}$ pint pastry cream : cream egg yolks with caster sugar until white ; add the flours and just enough cold milk to make a smooth paste.

If flavouring cream with chocolate, simmer 2-3 oz in remaining milk until melted, pour on to egg mixture, blend and return to pan ; stir over gentle heat until boiling.

Watchpoint Make sure that the pastry cream is smooth before letting it boil. If lumps form as it thickens, draw pan off heat, beat cream until smooth ; if too stiff, add extra milk.

Whip egg white until stiff, turn a little of boiling cream into a bowl and fold in egg white. Put this in pan and stir carefully over heat for about 3 minutes to set egg white. Turn cream into a bowl to cool.

If flavouring with coffee essence, add about 1 tablespoon to cooled cream.

Chocolate profiteroles

choux pastry for 4-6 people
(see opposite)
½ pint chocolate pastry cream
(see opposite)

For rich chocolate sauce
(sauce Suchard)
6 oz dessert, or bitter, chocolate
½ pint water
4 oz granulated sugar

Forcing bag ; plain éclair nozzle

Method
Set oven at 400°F or Mark 6.
Prepare choux pastry (see basic
recipe). Pipe out into small balls
or put out with a teaspoon on a
dampened baking sheet. Bake
for 20-30 minutes on a rising
temperature until crisp. Lift profiteroles off sheets, prick sides
to release steam. Leave to cool.

Prepare chocolate pastry
cream and set aside.

Meanwhile make chocolate
sauce : break up the chocolate
and melt in a pan with the water
over a slow heat ; when smooth
add the sugar. When sugar is
dissolved, bring to the boil and
simmer with lid off pan for about
10-15 minutes until sauce is
rich, syrupy and of a coating
consistency. Allow to cool.

Make a slit in the profiteroles
and fill with chocolate cream.
Pile them up in a pyramid in a
serving dish, spoon over sauce.

Griestorte with pears

6 eggs
8 oz caster sugar
juice and grated rind of 1 lemon
4 oz fine semolina
1 oz ground almonds

For filling
½-¾ pint double cream
1 teaspoon caster sugar
2-3 drops of vanilla essence
6 ripe dessert pears

To finish
icing sugar
chocolate (finely grated) —
    optional

Two 8-inch diameter sandwich tins

In this light but short-textured cake fine semolina is used instead of flour. This cake keeps better than a sponge and marries well with different fruits. The proportions given make two separate cakes, each serving 8.

Method
Butter the bottom of the sandwich tins and line each one with a disc of greaseproof paper; butter the greaseproof paper and sides of the tins, dust first with caster sugar and then with flour. Set the oven at 350°F or Mark 4.

Separate egg whites from yolks; work yolks and sugar together in a wooden bowl spoon until light in colour. Then add lemon juice and continue beating until thick. Stir in grated lemon rind, semolina and ground almonds. Whisk egg whites in a bowl to a firm snow and fold into mixture with a metal spoon. Turn into prepared tins, bake in pre-set oven for 40-50 minutes.

If using an electric mixer, the best result is obtained by beating together the yolks,

sugar and lemon juice until very thick. Stir in the dry ingredients as above and leave mixture standing while egg whites are whisked by hand with a balloon whisk. This short 'soaking time' of the semolina stops any grittiness in the finished cake.

Owing to the high proportion of egg to starch, the mixture rises a great deal but also subsides. This is quite in order but do not open the oven door until the cake has been baking for at least 25-30 minutes.

When the cakes are cold, split and fill with sweetened whipped cream, flavoured with vanilla essence, and sliced pears. Dust tops with icing sugar, and decorate with finely-grated chocolate.

Fill griestorte with sweetened, whipped cream and sliced pears

Fruit and jellies

There are many winter fruits that do not receive the attention they deserve. Even in winter we do not always want a rich filling pudding; if the first and main courses of a meal are particularly substantial, it is often a refreshing surprise to be served a light and delicious fruit or jelly. It is also a treat these days to be served a real home-made jelly instead of something made from a packet of jelly squares — these, although immeasurably useful, cannot give a dessert the depth of flavour provided by the 'real thing'.

A clear jelly, the basic lemon jelly for instance, should be absolutely crystal-clear and should literally 'shiver' — be barely set. Jellies that are too stiff are unpalatable.

The only special equipment you will require will be a flannel jelly bag and a stand, which you can improvise using two chair backs. Milk or wine jellies, and those made with oranges and some fruits, are left uncleared in the interests of flavour. For an uncleared jelly, a jelly bag is not necessary; straining through a linen tea towel, scalded thoroughly, is sufficient.

When making a clear jelly, it is best to clear 2 pints of liquid, which is enough for 4 people; any left over keeps well.

Turning out moulds

There is an art in turning a jelly out of its mould without spoiling its shape. For small moulds, have ready a bowl of hand-hot water, a sheet of greaseproof paper dampened with cold water, a palette knife and the prepared serving dish. Take up the mould, gripping it firmly with the palm of your hand over the top. Gently swish it through the water once or twice. Then, still holding the mould, turn it over so that your palm is underneath and the mould on top. Sharply knock the mould with the fingers of your other hand until the contents drop on to your open palm. Slide the jelly gently on to the dampened paper before transfering on to the serving dish with a palette knife.

For larger moulds, the procedure is much the same but here you lower the mould into the water until it just reaches the top edge. Leave for a few seconds, easing the jelly sideways gently with your fingers to make sure it is loose. Lift out the mould and dab away any water with a cloth. Hold serving dish over mould, then quickly turn it over. Set dish on table and, holding both mould and dish firmly together, give a sharp shake sideways. The jelly will drop on to the dish. Lift off the mould carefully and wipe round the edge of the dish before serving.

To display your jellies, or any foods coated with jelly, to their fullest advantage, serve them on stainless steel or silver dishes, or on plain white china with perhaps a gold edge, rather than anything patterned.

Setting agents

Gelatine The best is obtained from simmering calves feet in water and is especially delicate in flavour. Most powdered gelatine is obtained from the bones or tissues of animals or fish by boiling. Always use a good quality gelatine.

Agar-agar is prepared from seaweed and is used in vegetarian cookery and by people who do not wish to mix milk with animal proteins.

Isinglass comes from the swimming bladder of the sturgeon and is one of the purest forms of gelatine. It is more expensive than the powdered or French leaf gelatine.

Proportion needed to set 2 pints of liquid

Powdered gelatine	$\frac{3}{4}$-2 oz
French leaf gelatine	$1\frac{3}{4}$-2 oz
Strip gelatine	$1\frac{1}{2}$ oz
Agar-agar	$\frac{1}{2}$ oz
Isinglass	1 oz

Quantities given in the recipes are for powdered gelatine. As the setting strength of brands varies, it is essential to check with manufacturers' directions that you are using the correct amount.

Lemon jelly

1¾ oz gelatine
1½ pints water
pared rind of 3 lemons
7½ fl oz lemon juice
2 sticks cinnamon
7 oz lump sugar
whites and shells (wiped and
    lightly crushed) of 2 eggs
2½ fl oz sherry, or water

This basic recipe makes 2 pints of lemon jelly.

Method
Soak gelatine in $\frac{1}{4}$ pint of the water. Scald a large enamel pan, or an aluminium one with a ground base (use 6 pints capacity pan to allow for boiling). Pour in remaining $1\frac{1}{4}$ pints of water, add the lemon rind and juice, cinnamon and sugar; warm over gentle heat until sugar is dissolved.

Whip egg whites to a froth, add to the pan with the shells, gelatine and sherry, or water.

Whisk until liquid reaches boiling point, with a backwards (the reverse of the usual whisking movement) and downwards movement. Stop whisking at once and allow liquid to rise well in the pan. At once turn off heat or draw pan aside and leave liquid to settle for about 5 minutes. Bring liquid to the boil two more times, without whisking and drawing pan aside between each boiling to allow it to settle.

By this time a 'filter', or thick white crust, will have formed on top of the liquid. It will be cracked, so that the liquid below is visible. If the liquid is clear, carry on to the next stage; if it is muddy-looking, bring it to the boil once more.

Have ready a scalded jelly bag with a bowl underneath and turn the contents of the pan into it. Once the jelly begins to run through, take up the bowl (placing another underneath) and pour jelly back into the bag. After a few times the jelly running through should be crystal clear. Then allow it to run through completely before moving bag or bowl. A screw-top jar or jug of hot water placed in the bag helps to keep the jelly liquid.

Watchpoint Lump sugar is best for jelly-making; it will give a more brilliant jelly as it is less adulterated than the powdered sugar.

Fruit jelly madeleine

about 1¼ pints lemon jelly (see page
    127)
fresh fruit (black grapes, oranges,
    or pineapple
For vanilla cream
2 egg yolks
1 dessertspoon caster sugar
¼ pint milk
3-4 tablespoons water
¼ oz gelatine
2-3 drops of vanilla essence
3¾ fl oz double cream (lightly
    whipped)

*Charlotte tin, or glass bowl (about
1¾-2 pints capacity)*

Method
Have ready the tin or bowl. Pour
in cold jelly to cover base by
¼-½ inch. Arrange the fruit on
this and set with a little jelly and
put aside.

To prepare the vanilla cream:
cream the yolks with the sugar,
scald the milk, pour on to the
eggs, return to pan, thicken
over heat without boiling. Add
the water to the gelatine and,
when soft, dissolve over a
gentle heat. Add to the custard
with a few drops of vanilla.

When custard is cool and on
the point of setting, fold in the
whipped cream. Pour mixture
carefully on to the jellied fruit
and leave to set. Add any leftover fruit to remaining jelly and
spoon over the top to fill the tin
or bowl completely.

Leave madeleine for 1-2
hours, then turn out and sur-
round with chopped jelly.

Port wine jelly

1 pint port wine (about ¾ bottle)
½-inch piece stick of cinnamon
2 strips of lemon rind
4 oz lump sugar
3 tablespoons gelatine (soaked in
    ¾ pint water)

*Jelly mould (decorative china may
be used, or, traditionally, tin-lined
copper)*

Method
Pour half the port into a
scrupulously clean saucepan.
Bring to the boil, simmer 2-3
minutes, then add flavourings
and sugar. Set aside to infuse
for 10 minutes.

Soak gelatine in the water,
leave 2-3 minutes, then pour
into the pan containing the
flavoured port. Heat gently to
dissolve gelatine, then add rest
of port. Strain, pour into jelly
mould (previously rinsed out in
cold water) and leave to set.
Dip mould into warm water to
turn out the jelly.

Milk jelly

1½ pints creamy milk
pared rind of 1 lemon
3 tablespoons gelatine (soaked in
    ¼ pint water)
¼ pint cream

Jelly mould

Method
Heat lemon rind in milk, then
leave to infuse for 7-10 minutes.
Soak gelatine in water for 2-3
minutes. Add to milk and stir
until dissolved. Strain into jelly
mould (previously rinsed out in
cold water), leave to set. Turn
out, pour the cream round
before serving.

Plum compote with rich almond cake

1 lb red plums
1 wineglass red wine, or port
4 tablespoons redcurrant jelly
grated rind and juice of 1 orange

Method

Pour wine into a pan large enough to take the plums, boil until reduced to half the quantity. Add redcurrant jelly, stir gently until dissolved, then add the orange rind and juice.

Halve and stone the plums and put rounded side down (cut side uppermost) in the pan; let syrup boil up and over fruit, then poach gently until fruit is quite tender. Allow a full 10 minutes for this, even if the fruit is ripe.

Turn fruit into a bowl to cool; serve with a rich almond cake, or creamed rice.

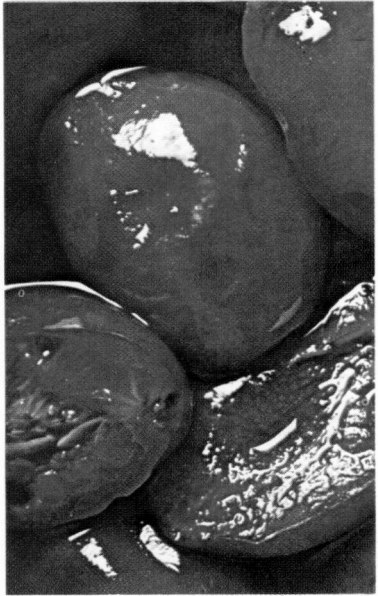

Rich almond cake

4 oz butter
5 oz caster sugar
3 eggs
3 oz ground almonds
1½ oz flour
2-3 drops of almond essence

Deep 7-inch diameter sandwich tin

Method

Grease and flour sandwich tin, cover base with disc of grease-proof paper; set the oven at 350°F or Mark 4.

Soften butter with a wooden spoon in a bowl, add the sugar a tablespoon at a time and beat thoroughly until mixture is soft and light. Add the eggs, one at a time, adding one-third of the almonds with each egg. Beat well. Fold in the flour and almond essence with a metal spoon and turn cake mixture into the prepared tin.

Bake in pre-set oven for 45-50 minutes until cake is cooked. (Test by inserting a thin skewer; it should come out clean.) When cooked, the cake should also shrink very slightly from the sides of the tin.

To turn out, have ready two wire cooling racks, put a clean folded tea towel or single thickness of absorbent paper on one of them. Loosen the sides of the cake with a round-bladed knife, place the rack with the towel or paper on top of the cake (towel next to it) and turn over; remove the tin and disc of paper from the base.

Place second rack on top of cake base and carefully and quickly turn it over again. This prevents the rack marking top of cake. Dust top with caster sugar.

Fruit jelly tart

4 oz quantity of French flan
  pastry (see method, page 14)

For fruit jelly
1-1½ pints lemon jelly (see page 127)
fruit in season (eg. black and white
  grapes, bananas, segments of
  tangerine)

For pastry cream
1 rounded dessertspoon custard
  powder
¼ pint milk
¼ pint double cream (whipped)
1 dessertspoon caster sugar

*7-inch diameter flan ring ; 6-inch
  diameter sandwich tin*

This is a pretty and decorative
sweet — especially for a buffet,
lunch or supper. This quantity
is sufficient for 4-5 people but
may, of course, be made larger
if wished. Remember that the
sandwich tin must be slightly
smaller than the flan case so
that the jelly fits snugly on top
of the cream filling.

Method
Roll out the pastry and use to
line flan ring; bake blind and
remove pastry when cool.
Watchpoint Pastry should
be made up and chilled for at
least 1 hour before baking.

Take up sandwich tin and
pour in enough cool jelly to
cover the bottom to a depth of
½ inch ; leave it to set. Arrange
the chosen fruit on this and set
in position with 2-3 tablespoons of cool jelly. Repeat
with another layer of fruit and
fill to the brim of the tin with
remaining cool jelly ; leave to set.

To prepare pastry cream : mix
the custard powder to a paste
with the milk in a saucepan.
Stir over heat until it boils.
Turn into a basin, whisk well
and cover with wet greaseproof paper to prevent a skin
forming. When the custard is
quite cold, fold in the whipped
cream and the sugar. Spread
this cream on the bottom of the
flan case.

Dip the base and sides of the
sandwich tin in warm water
and turn out carefully on to
the cream in the flan case. Chill
tart slightly before serving.

Turning the fruit jelly on to the pastry cream in the flan case

This fruit jelly tart contains rings of grapes and bananas ; use any seasonal fruits

Banana chartreuse

1½ pints lemon jelly (see page 127)
about 12 pistachio nuts
    (blanched) — optional
3 bananas

Ring mould (1¼-1½ pints capacity)

Method

Have ready the jelly, which should be cool but not set. Stand the mould in a roasting tin, pour round a little cold water and add a few ice cubes.

Turn the jelly into a bowl, stand this in water with ice cubes and stir gently with a metal spoon until the jelly is cold to the touch but not set. Spoon in enough jelly to cover the bottom of the mould to a depth of $\frac{1}{4}$-$\frac{1}{2}$ inch. Leave to set.

Blanch and finely chop the pistachio nuts. Slice bananas. Place nuts on a layer of jelly, pour a little more over, and when set arrange a single layer of bananas on the top, set this with a little more jelly and repeat this process until mould is full, the last layer being of jelly. Leave for at least 1½-2 hours to set. Then turn out chartreuse and fill the centre with chopped jelly.

Serve a bowl of whipped cream separately.

Putting chopped pistachio nuts on to the layer of set jelly at the bottom of the ring mould

Placing banana slices, first dipped in jelly to help them stick, in layers above the nuts

Banana chartreuse, with banana and pistachio nuts arranged carefully in the jelly, and whipped cream served separately

Pineapple mousse en surprise

3 eggs
2 egg yolks
3 oz caster sugar
$\frac{1}{2}$ oz gelatine
2 tablespoons cold water
juice of 1 lemon
$\frac{1}{4}$ pint double cream
1 egg white
$\frac{1}{4}$ pint canned pineapple juice
(not syrup)

For garnish
1 small can pineapple
12 ratafias, or 4 almond
macaroons (see page 154)
2 tablespoons kirsch, or juice
from the pineapple
1 small carton (about 3 fl oz) of
double cream (whipped)

*6-inch diameter top (No. 2 size)
soufflé dish ; 1 lb jam jar*

Ratafias are button-size macaroons, strongly-flavoured with
almonds.

Method

Prepare the soufflé dish by tying
a band of greaseproof paper
around it. Then stand a lightly
oiled jam jar in the centre.

Place the whole eggs and
yolks in a basin and whisk in
sugar gradually. Have ready a
pan of boiling water, remove it
from the stove, set the basin on
top and whisk until egg mousse
is very thick. If you have an
electric mixer, this heat will not
be necessary.

When egg mousse is very
thick, remove the bowl from the
saucepan and continue whisking
until it is quite cold (to speed the
process stand your bowl in cold
water containing a few ice cubes).

Soak gelatine in water and
add lemon juice ; dissolve gelatine in this liquid in pan over
gentle heat.

Whip $\frac{1}{4}$ pint cream lightly,
whisk egg white until stiff. Stir
cold pineapple juice and warm
gelatine into the mousse and,
as it begins to thicken, quickly
fold in the cream and egg white.
Pour the mixture into the prepared dish, drop 2-3 ice cubes
into jam jar to hold it in position
and to help mousse set quickly.
Put in refrigerator to set.

Drain the pineapple, cut in
small pieces and mix with the
ratafias or broken macaroons
and macerate (soak) with the
kirsch or juice.

When mousse is set, carefully
remove the jam jar and immediately fill mousse centre with
pineapple and ratafia mixture.
Remove the paper from the
soufflé dish and decorate the
mousse with whipped cream.

Watchpoint This mousse must
be made with a can of pineapple juice and never with the
juice of a fresh pineapple because this contains an enzyme
which destroys the setting power
of gelatine. We suggest using
canned pineapple for the centre,
knowing that many housewives
like to finish the sweet for a
party early in the day. Fresh
pineapple may be used for the
filling but it must be put in not
more than 1 hour before serving,
sprinkle it with sugar before
mixing with ratafias and kirsch.

Do not try to be economical
and use syrup from the canned
pineapple to make mousse ; it
would be too sweet and add
little or no true flavour of pineapple.

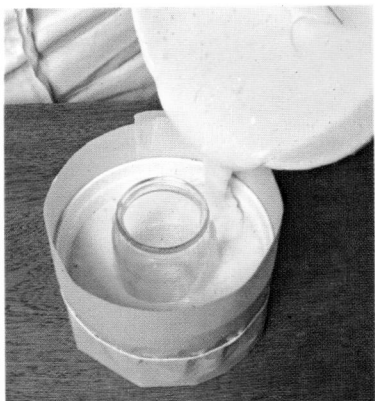

Pouring pineapple mousse into the prepared soufflé dish

Filling the mousse with pineapple and crushed ratafias

Pears Cassis

4-6 ripe dessert pears (2 over
for second helpings)
6 tablespoons granulated sugar
½ pint water
1 vanilla pod, or 2-3 drops of
vanilla essence
1 small can blackcurrants
(about 7½ fl oz)
1 dessertspoon arrowroot
caster sugar (for dusting)

Method

Dissolve the sugar in pan of water, add the vanilla pod, boil for 5 minutes, remove vanilla pod, draw aside; if using vanilla essence, add it at this stage.

Peel and halve the pears, scoop out the core with the point of a teaspoon and put pears straight into the pan of syrup, rounded side down. Bring syrup to the boil, letting it boil right up and over the fruit, then lower the heat. Cover the pan and leave pears to simmer very gently until they look almost transparent. Leave them to cool in the covered pan. Rub the blackcurrants through a fine strainer or work to a purée in a liquidiser, measure and make quantity up to ¾ pint with syrup from the pears; then tip into a pan and heat gently.

Mix the arrowroot with 2 tablespoons pear syrup, add to the blackcurrant mixture and stir until boiling.

Drain pears, put into a serving dish and pour over blackcurrant sauce, dust the top with caster sugar to prevent a skin forming and leave to cool.

Pears belle Hélène

4-5 even-size pears
syrup (made with 1 pint water and
4 oz sugar)
1 vanilla pod (split)

For Suchard sauce
6 oz block chocolate
½ pint water
3 oz granulated sugar
4 lumps of sugar (optional)
1 orange (optional)

Method

Dissolve sugar in water in a shallow pan and boil rapidly for 2 minutes. Peel the pears and carefully core them from the flower end. Lift them into the syrup, add vanilla pod, cover pan and poach gently for 20-30 minutes until tender. Cool in the syrup.

To prepare Suchard sauce: rub the sugar lumps over the orange until they are well soaked with the oil from the zest. Break up the chocolate and add it to the water in a pan. Simmer until chocolate is dissolved, then add the granulated sugar; simmer with pan uncovered until the sauce is syrupy and will coat the back of the spoon. Draw pan aside (add the sugar lumps if used). Stir, reboil and pour sauce off to cool. To serve, drain the pears thoroughly, dish them up and coat with the Suchard sauce.

Note : when poaching the pears, the rind of the orange can be pared and added to the syrup in place of the vanilla pod.

Pears belle Hélène, coated with a rich Suchard chocolate sauce

Apricot suédoise with meringues

½ lb dried apricots, soaked overnight in 1½ pints boiling water
strip of lemon rind
4 oz granulated sugar
1 rounded tablespoon gelatine
¼ pint water
½ pint double cream

For meringues
2 egg whites
4 oz caster sugar
vanilla flavouring

6-inch diameter (No. 2 size) soufflé dish, or cake tin

Suédoise usually means a sweet fruit purée set with gelatine, put into a mould and served with cream or custard.

Method

Cook the apricots with the lemon rind in the liquid in which they were soaked until very soft, then rub through a sieve or strainer. Measure the purée and make up to 1½ pints with water. Return to the pan with the sugar and simmer 5-10 minutes. Soak the gelatine in the water and then dissolve over heat. Add to the fruit purée and allow to cool. Pour into a wet soufflé dish or cake tin and leave to set in refrigerator for several hours.

To prepare meringues: whisk egg whites until stiff. Whisk 1 dessertspoon of the sugar into the whites for 1 minute, or until the mixture looks like satin. Fold the remaining sugar in with a metal spoon.

Spoon blobs of mixture (about the size of a penny) on to a baking sheet lined with non-stick (silicone) cooking paper, and flick up mixture into peaks, or pipe into small meringues. Bake for 45 minutes in a low oven at 250°F or Mark ½ until dry and crisp.

Turn the jelly on to a serving dish and cover first with whipped cream flavoured with vanilla, then with meringues.

Oranges en surprise

5-6 large seedless oranges
4-6 oz glacé fruit
2-3 tablespoons Grand Marnier
2 egg quantity of meringue cuite
  (see page 64)
little caster sugar (for dusting)

Any glacé fruit that is around at Christmas time — including stem ginger, angelica and cherries — can be used. The liqueur can be omitted, but it does give a good flavour.

Method
Set the oven at 400°F or Mark 6. Slice or dice the glacé fruit and macerate pieces in the Grand Marnier. Slice off the flower end of the oranges and, using a grapefruit knife, scoop out the flesh. Take out the core, and remove as many membranes as possible. Mix the orange flesh with the glacé fruit and replace in the skins. Have ready the meringue and pipe this on each orange: place them in a roasting tin containing ice cubes. Dust with sugar and put into the pre-set hot oven until just coloured (about 5-10 minutes), then take out and serve cool.

Watchpoint The meringue should be browned quickly because if the oranges are allowed to cook in any way they will get a marmalade taste. The ice cubes in the roasting tin help to keep the oranges from cooking.

Top : putting a mixture of orange flesh and glacé fruit into one of the scooped out oranges for oranges en surprise
Above : piping on meringue before placing oranges in a tin of ice to keep them from cooking while meringue is browning

Oranges in caramel
with brandy snaps (see page 142)

8 large seedless oranges
(Navel are best)

For caramel
8 oz granulated sugar
¼ pint cold water
¼ pint warm water

8 cocktail sticks

Method

Put the sugar and cold water in a pan and dissolve sugar over a very gentle heat.

Watchpoint The rule for sugar boiling is to dissolve sugar slowly and boil steadily to prevent it crystallising, so keep the heat under the pan very low as the water should not boil until every grain of sugar has dissolved. Do not stir. The sugar can be moved from the bottom of the pan by drawing a spoon carefully through it.

When the sugar has dissolved, bring to the boil and then cook steadily to a rich brown caramel.

Hold the pan over a bowl of lukewarm water so that the base just touches water (to prevent further cooking). Cover the hand holding the saucepan with a cloth (mixture may splash and scald) and quickly pour in warm water. Pour into a jug or a bowl and then leave to cool.

Pare a little rind from 1 orange using a potato peeler, cut into needle-like shreds, cook for 1 minute in boiling water, then drain and dry.

Cut the rind, pith and first membrane from the oranges leaving the flesh exposed. This is best done with a serrated-edge knife and, if you cut round with a sawing action, you should not lose any juice.

Hold each orange at top and bottom in your hand over a bowl and cut across in slices. Hold these slices together with a cocktail stick; arrange in a deep glass dish, pour caramel on top, sprinkle over the shredded orange rind and chill well.

*Below left : use a serrated-edge knife to remove peel and pith from oranges;
hold over a bowl, cut with a sawing action to avoid losing juice
After slicing the oranges, reshape and then secure slices in place with a
cocktail stick pour caramel over, sprinkle orange rind and chill*

Brandy snaps

(see photograph on page 141)

4 oz butter
4 oz demerara sugar
4 oz golden syrup
4 oz plain flour
pinch of salt
1 teaspoon ground ginger
1 teaspoon lemon juice
2-3 drops of vanilla essence

This quantity makes about 20, and $\frac{1}{4}$ pint of double cream will fill 8-12 brandy snaps, enough for a dinner party.

Method

Set the oven at 325°F or Mark 3. Put the butter, sugar and syrup into a saucepan and heat gently until the butter has melted and sugar dissolved. Leave to cool slightly. Sift flour with salt and ginger into mixture, stir well, adding lemon juice and vanilla essence.

Put teaspoons of mixture on a wellgreased baking sheet at least 4 inches apart and cook in pre-set oven for 8 minutes. Leave biscuits for 2-3 minutes, then remove from the tin with a sharp knife, turn over and roll round the handle of a wooden spoon. Store in an airtight tin as soon as they are cold. Serve, filled with whipped cream, with the oranges in caramel.

Left : when baking brandy snaps, put only a teaspoon of mixture on the baking sheet ; leave room for expansion between spoonfuls
Right : before the brandy snaps get too cold, roll them up on the handle of a wooden spoon

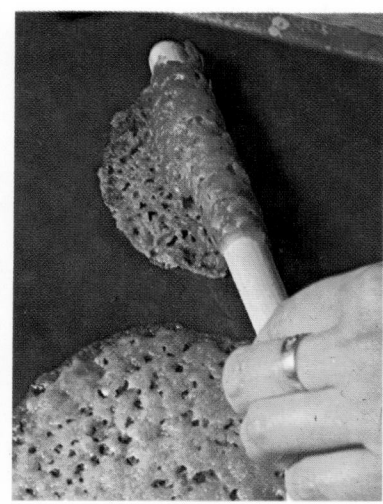

Sauces

A glance at the recipes earlier in this book will reveal how many really delicious puddings need a sauce to complete them.

Good sauces are rich, smooth, glossy, and the flavour is concentrated. A little goes a long way so, though it may be a temptation to be generous with so delicious a concoction, it is important not to drown the pudding itself. The result could be over-rich and unpalatable.

The English are said not to be at their best when making sweet sauces. There is a tendency to serve watered down jam for fruit sauce, and a sickly cocoa mixture for chocolate sauce. The French, on the other hand, are particularly renowned for their sauces. This branch of cooking is one of the most vital facets of their art. In fact there need be no mystique about sauce-making; it's just very important to measure the ingredients exactly, because if those are wrong, no amount of cooking will give the right consistency.

It is important that the sauce complement the flavour of the dish it accompanies. If the pud-

ding is tart, tone it down with a bland, slightly sweet sauce. If the pudding itself has only a delicate flavour, it will need a sauce that has the faintest piquancy. If the pudding is rich, it will need a rich sauce to keep pace with it and enhance the flavour.

Unlike many savoury sauces, sweet ones are not made on standard basic recipes; each is an individual sauce. Many dessert sauces are contrived to go especially with one pudding, however, you may often be able to make an acceptable dessert out of leftover cake served with a really delicious sauce. But remember it is important to eat a sauce as it is meant to be — if it is meant to be hot, eat it hot; if it is meant to be cold, eat it cold.

There is certain equipment that will help you perfect your sauce — a small, heavy saucepan is usually the best to use for hot sauces, and a balloon whisk will help you get the maximum out of whisked mixtures, and ensure that there are no lumps present.

Some of the butter foundation

sauces are known as 'hard' sauces — for the obvious reason that they are left to solidify before use. These are particularly delicious with Christmassy puddings like plum pudding or mince pie. The fact that they are often flavoured with spirits — notably brandy and rum — has no connection with the name 'hard' !

For this book we have tried to confine ourselves to fruit sauces made with fruits that will be in season in winter. For those cooks who make preserving one of their summer de-lights, bottled fruit will help to ring the changes.

Note A number of sweet sauces are made with egg. The most important thing to remember when preparing these is that the sauces must not boil once the egg has been added. It often helps to prepare it in a basin held over a pan of simmering water, rather than directly in a saucepan.

For jam or syrup sauces, the consistency depends on evaporating the sugar and water to a syrup — but take care not to let it form crystals.

Hot sabayon sauce

Put 3 egg yolks, 1 tablespoon caster sugar, $\frac{1}{4}$ pint sherry and a small strip of lemon rind into a small basin and stand on a small saucepan containing a little simmering water. Whisk until sauce becomes very frothy and starts to thicken. Remove lemon rind and serve at once.

Sabayon is the French corruption of zabaione (or zabaglione), the Italian sweet which can be served as a sauce for a pudding, or on its own in a warmed glass, with Savoy fingers or thin slices of sponge cake baked in the oven until dry and crisp. In Italy this is made with Marsala or white wine instead of sherry.

This is the frothy consistency of sabayon sauce after whisking over boiling water

Cold sabayon sauce

2 oz granulated sugar
2$\frac{1}{2}$ fl oz water
2 egg yolks
grated rind and juice of $\frac{1}{2}$
   lemon
1 tablespoon rum, or brandy, or
   2 tablespoons golden sherry
$\frac{1}{4}$ pint double cream

Serve over fresh or sugared fruit, apple charlotte and other fruit puddings.

Method
Dissolve the sugar gently in the water, and then boil the sugar until the cooled syrup will form a thread between your finger and thumb. Put the egg yolks into a bowl, beat well and take the syrup off the heat, allow the bubbles to subside and pour on to the yolks, whisking well. Whisk the mixture until thick, add the grated lemon rind and juice.

Flavour with the rum, brandy or sherry and continue to whisk for 1-2 minutes. Whisk the cream until it will just hold its shape, fold it into sauce and chill.

Mousseline sauce

1 egg
1 egg yolk
1$\frac{1}{2}$ oz caster sugar
2 tablespoons sherry, or fruit
   juice

Serve with steamed, or baked sponge, puddings.

Method
Put all the ingredients together in a bowl. Whisk over a pan of simmering water until mixture is thick and frothy.

Suchard sauce

6 oz plain block chocolate
good $\frac{1}{2}$ pint water
4 oz sugar
1 vanilla pod (split)

Serve this sauce with rich sweets such as ice-cream and chocolate profiteroles.

Method
Put the water and the sugar together into a pan, dissolve over gentle heat and add the vanilla pod. Simmer for 4-5 minutes then remove pod.
 Melt the chocolate on a plate over a pan of warm water, discard the water, and put the chocolate into the pan, then beat in the sugar syrup, a little at a time. Simmer until it is a thick rich syrup. Use hot or cold.

Chocolate sauce 1

1 tablespoon cocoa
2 tablespoons granulated sugar
$\frac{1}{2}$ pint water
2-3 drops of vanilla essence

Method
Put the cocoa and sugar in a deep saucepan, mix smoothly with the water and then bring slowly to the boil, stirring from time to time. Simmer gently for 10 minutes, then add the vanilla essence. The sauce is now ready to serve.

Chocolate sauce 2

2 oz plain block chocolate
2 tablespoons sugar
1 teaspoon cocoa
1 teaspoon instant coffee
$\frac{1}{2}$ pint water
1 egg yolk (optional)
$\frac{1}{2}$ teaspoon vanilla essence

Method
Break up the chocolate and put into a saucepan with the sugar, cocoa, coffee and water. Heat slowly, stirring frequently until dissolved. Then simmer with the lid off the pan until it is the consistency of thin cream.
 Draw pan aside, and if using the yolk, blend with 1-2 table-spoons of the hot sauce before adding it to the pan, and then add the vanilla essence. If no yolk is used, continue to sim-mer the sauce until it is a little thicker before adding vanilla.

Red wine sauce

1 tablespoon granulated sugar
$\frac{1}{4}$ pint of water
2 tablespoons red jam
rind of $\frac{1}{4}$ lemon
1 teaspoon arrowroot (slaked
   with 1 tablespoon water)
2 tablespoons claret

Serve with baked vanilla soufflé (see page 69).

Method
Place the sugar, water, jam and lemon rind in the pan and slowly bring to the boil. Simmer gently for about 8 minutes, then thicken with the slaked arrow-root. Cook until clear, add the wine, strain and serve hot.

Banana sauce

1 banana (finely sliced)
juice of $\frac{1}{2}$ lemon (made up to
   8 fl oz with water)
1 tablespoon maraschino, or
   juice from maraschino cherries
1 oz granulated sugar
1 dessertspoon arrowroot

Serve with vanilla ice-cream
or castle puddings.

Method
Put the lemon juice, water and
maraschino, or juice, into a pan
with the sugar and dissolve over
gentle heat. Mix the arrowroot
smoothly with 1 tablespoon
water, stir into the pan and boil
until clear. Add the sliced
banana and serve hot.

Caramel sauce

6 oz granulated sugar
2$\frac{1}{2}$ fl oz cold water
$\frac{1}{4}$ pint warm water

Serve either plain or with one
sliced banana added to it, with
a squeeze of lemon juice also
added just before serving. It is
also good served with little
choux, when filled with cream
or vanilla bavarois.

Method
Dissolve the sugar slowly in the
cold water, then boil rapidly
until a good caramel. Draw
aside, add the warm water
carefully then stir over heat until
dissolved, then boil rapidly until
syrupy, ie. the consistency of
thin cream. Pour off and cool.
If it thickens too much on
cooling add 1-2 tablespoons
warm water. Serve when cold.

Lemon butter

3 oz unsalted butter
grated rind of 1 lemon
2 oz caster, or icing, sugar
juice of $\frac{1}{2}$ lemon

Method
Soften the butter in a bowl with
the grated rind of the lemon,
add the caster or icing sugar a
little at a time with the juice of
half the lemon and beat mixture
until light and fluffy. Pile into a
small dish and leave until very
firm before serving.

Hot fudge sauce

3 oz soft light brown sugar
1 tablespoon golden syrup
½ pint milk
2 oz butter
½ vanilla pod (split)
2 teaspoons arrowroot (slaked with 1 tablespoon water)

Method

Put the sugar and syrup in a heavy pan and dissolve over gentle heat. In another saucepan heat the milk with the butter and vanilla, and leave it to infuse.

After about 10 minutes, when milk is well flavoured with vanilla, remove the pod from pan. Boil the sugar mixture until caramelised, then add the milk mixture, stirring until the lumps are dissolved, beat until smooth. Add slaked arrowroot, and boil for 1 minute. Serve at once.

Hot fudge sauce is good poured over coffee ice-cream

Brandy butter

(Senior Wrangler sauce)

4 oz unsalted butter
4 oz caster sugar
2-3 tablespoons brandy (to
    taste)

This butter is good with plum pudding and mince pies.

Method

Cream the butter thoroughly, beat in the sugar by degrees and continue to beat until white. Then beat in the brandy, a teaspoon at a time. Pile up in a small dish or bowl and chill until firm.

> **Senior Wrangler** is a title dating from 1750, given to Cambridge undergraduates who passed first class in their Mathematics Tripos. The name was given · to brandy butter by a forebear of Rosemary Hume, Dr. Whewell, who was a Second Wrangler and Master of Trinity in the mid-19th century.

Rum butter

3 oz unsalted butter
3 oz soft brown sugar
grated rind of $\frac{1}{2}$ lemon and
    squeeze of juice
2-3 tablespoons of rum

This hard sauce is excellent with plum pudding and mince pies. In Cumberland it is served at christening parties.

Method

Cream the butter thoroughly, add the sugar gradually with the lemon rind and juice. Continue to beat, adding the rum gradually to flavour the butter well. Pile up in a small dish and chill before serving.

Rum sauce

4 oz sugar
$\frac{1}{2}$ cup water
dark Jamaica rum (to taste)
1 teaspoon lemon, or fresh lime,
    juice

Serve with rich fruit puddings.

Method

Dissolve the sugar in the water, bring to the boil and boil for 5 minutes. Add dark Jamaica rum to taste, with 1 teaspoon lemon juice, but if obtainable fresh lime juice is even better.

Melba sauce

1½ lb fresh raspberries, or frozen
ones without sugar.
4 tablespoons icing sugar
(sifted)

Method
If using frozen raspberries buy
them 2-3 days before wanted
and leave them to thaw in
refrigerator. Pick over fresh
raspberries. Rub the raspberries
through a nylon strainer and
then beat in the sifted icing
sugar, 1 tablespoon at a time.

Butterscotch sauce

1 tablespoon golden syrup
½ oz butter
2 tablespoons demerara sugar
½ pint warm water
squeeze of lemon juice
1 dessertspoon custard powder
(slaked with 1 tablespoon
water)

Serve with ice-cream.

Method
Put the syrup, butter and sugar
into a pan and cook to a rich
brown toffee. Draw aside, add
the water carefully and then
lemon juice. Boil up sauce
and pour on to slaked custard
powder — reboil to thicken and
cook custard.

Apricot sauce

Soak about ¼ lb dried apricots
overnight then simmer in the
soaking liquor, with a strip of
lemon rind, until tender. Then
rub apricots through a strainer
or sieve. Sweeten to taste and
thin sauce a little with water, if
necessary.

Apricot jam, red jam, or marmalade, sauce

2 rounded tablespoons of home-
made apricot, or red, jam, or
marmalade
about 7½ fl oz water
2 strips of lemon rind (if using
apricot jam, or marmalade)
1 tablespoon sugar
1 tablespoon arrowroot (slaked
with 1 tablespoon water) —
optional

Serve with sponges and other
baked, or steamed, puddings.

Method
Put all the ingredients, except
the arrowroot, into a pan and
bring slowly to the boil, stirring
well. Taste, and if not strong
enough in flavour add a little
more jam or marmalade. Continue to simmer for 5-6 minutes,
then remove the lemon rind and
thicken if necessary with the
arrowroot. Serve hot.

Apricot jam sauce with rum

4 tablespoons smooth apricot
  jam
2 tablespoons water
juice of $\frac{1}{2}$ lemon
1 tablespoon rum

Method
Put the jam, water and lemon juice into a pan and heat gently to melt the jam; bring to the boil. Remove from the heat and add the rum. Strain sauce into a bowl and serve cold.

Pineapple sauce

$\frac{1}{4}$ cut crushed pineapple, or 1 small
  can crushed pineapple
3 dessertspoons caster sugar
1 dessertspoon cornflour
pinch of salt
$\frac{3}{4}$ cup unsweetened pineapple
  juice
1 teaspoon lemon juice

Method
Mix the sugar, cornflour and salt together. Add the pineapple juice and cook for 5 minutes. Add the lemon juice and then the crushed pineapple.

Walnut and apple sauce

1 oz walnut kernels (coarsely
  chopped)
1 lb cooking apples
$\frac{1}{2}$ oz butter
pared rind of $\frac{1}{2}$ lemon
3 oz sugar
$\frac{1}{2}$ cup water

This is served with either ice-cream, caramel bavarois or rice pudding.

Method
Rub the butter round a sauté pan. Wipe the apples, quarter, core and slice into the pan. Add lemon rind, cover apples with a piece of foil or greaseproof paper and then put on lid and cook over gentle heat to a pulp. Rub through a strainer. Rinse out the pan, then boil sugar and water for about 3-4 minutes, until it is a thick syrup, then draw aside and stir in the pulp. Return the pan to the heat and simmer the mixture until it is the consistency of cream.

Add the walnuts to the sauce. Cook for 1 minute then draw aside. Serve either hot or cold.

Orange cream sauce

1 large, or 2 small, oranges
5 lumps of sugar
¼ pint double cream (lightly whipped)

For custard
¼ pint milk
1 teaspoon caster sugar
2 egg yolks (mixed with 1 teaspoon arrowroot)

Method
First make the custard, and leave to get cold. Thinly pare rind from half the orange with a potato peeler, cut into fine shreds and simmer until tender. Drain well and set them aside for decoration.

Rub the lump sugar over the second half of orange to remove all the zest — each lump should be completely saturated with the oil from the skin. Place these lumps in a small basin, strain the juice from the oranges and pour 5 tablespoons of this juice over the sugar lumps, stir until the sugar is dissolved. Stir the orange syrup into the cream and the cold custard, together with fine shreds of orange rind.

Rich orange cream sauce

grated rind and juice of 3 oranges (to give ¼ pint)
juice of 1 lemon
4 oz granulated sugar
2 oz unsalted butter
2 eggs (well beaten)
1 carton double cream (3-4 fl oz) — lightly whipped

Serve with Eve's pudding (see page 35).

Method
Put all the ingredients in a pudding basin (except the cream). Stand the basin in a pan of boiling water (or use a double boiler), then stir the mixture gently over a low heat until it is thick.

Watchpoint Do not let the sauce get too hot, otherwise it will curdle.

When the sauce is quite cold fold in the cream.

Appendix

Notes and basic recipes

Baking blind

1 A flan case should be pre-cooked before filling with soft or cooked fruit. Once the flan ring is lined with pastry, chill for about 30 minutes to ensure the dough is well set.

2 Now line the pastry with crumpled greaseproof paper, pressing it well into the dough at the bottom edge and sides.

3 Three-parts fill the flan with uncooked rice or beans (to hold the shape) and put into the oven to bake. An 8-inch diameter flan ring holding a 6-8 oz. quantity of pastry should cook for about 26 minutes in an oven at 400°F or Mark 6.

4 After about 20 minutes of the cooking time take flan out of the oven and carefully remove the paper and rice, or beans. (Beans may be used many times over for baking blind.) Replace the flan in the oven to complete cooking. The ring itself can either be taken off with the paper and rice, or removed after cooking. Once cooked, slide the flan on to a wire rack and then leave to cool.

Breadcrumbs

To make crumbs : take a large loaf (the best type to use is a sandwich loaf) at least two days old. Cut off the crust and keep to one side. Break up bread into crumbs either by rubbing through a wire sieve or a Mouli sieve, or by working in an electric blender.

Spread crumbs on to a sheet of paper laid on a baking tin and cover with another sheet of paper to keep off any dust. Leave to dry in a warm temperature — the plate rack, or warming drawer, or the top of the oven, or even the airing cupboard, is ideal. The crumbs may take a day or two to dry thoroughly, and they must be crisp before storing in a jar. To make them uni-formly fine sift them through a wire bowl strainer.

To make browned crumbs : bake the crusts in a slow oven until golden-brown, then crush or grind through a mincer. Sift and store as for white crumbs. These browned ones are known as raspings and are used for any dish that is coated with a sauce and browned in the oven.

Gelatine

The best is obtained from simmering calves feet in water and is especially delicate in flavour. Most powdered gelatine is obtained from the bones or tissues of animals or fish by boiling. Always use a good quality gelatine and check the amount required with manufacturer's directions (see also page 126).

Macaroons

7 oz caster sugar
1 oz granulated sugar
4 oz ground almonds
$\frac{1}{2}$ oz rice flour
2-3 egg whites (according to size)
2-3 drops of vanilla essence
rice paper
split almonds

This makes approximately 9.

Method
Set oven at 350°F or Mark 4.

Mix the sugars, ground almonds and rice flour together in a mixing bowl ; add the egg whites and the essence and beat all together with a wooden spoon for about 5 minutes. Scrape down sides of bowl ; allow to stand for 5 minutes.

Meanwhile cut the rice paper into 3-inch squares and place, shiny side down, on a dry baking sheet. Continue beating the almond mixture for 5 minutes more until thick and white. Using a bag and $\frac{1}{4}$-inch pipe, shape neatly on to rice paper squares, place a split almond in centre of each macaroon, bake in pre-set oven for 20-30 minutes.

Nuts

To brown hazelnuts (already shelled) : do not blanch first but bake for 7-8 minutes in a moderate oven at 350°F or Mark 4, then rub briskly in a rough cloth to remove skin.

Almonds : buy them with their skins on. This way they retain their oil better. Blanching to remove the skins gives extra juiciness.

To blanch almonds : pour boiling water over the shelled nuts cover the pan and leave until cool. Then the skins can be easily removed (test one with finger and thumb). Drain, rinse in cold water; press skins off with fingers. Rinse, dry thoroughly.

To brown blanched almonds : bake as for hazelnuts.

To chop almonds : first blanch, skin, chop and then brown them in the oven if desired.

To shred almonds : first blanch, skin, split in two and cut each half lengthways in fine pieces. These can then be used as they are or browned quickly in oven, with or without a sprinkling of caster sugar.

To flake almonds : first blanch, skin, and cut horizontally into flakes with a small sharp knife.

To grind almonds : first blanch, skin, chop and pound into a paste (use a pestle and mortar, or a grinder, or the butt end of a rolling pin). Home-prepared ground almonds taste much better than the ready ground variety.

Redcurrant jelly

It is not possible to give a specific quantity of redcurrants as recipe is governed by amount of juice made.

Method

Wash fruit and, without removing from stems, put in a 7 lb jam jar or stone crock. Cover and stand in deep pan of hot water. Simmer on top of stove or in oven at 350°F or Mark 4, mashing the fruit from time to time, until all the juice is extracted (about 1 hour).

Then turn fruit into a jelly-bag, or double linen strainer, and allow to drain overnight over a basin.

Watchpoint To keep the jelly clear and sparkling, do not try to speed up draining process by forcing juice through ; this will cloud jelly.

Measure juice. Allowing 1 lb lump, or preserving, sugar to each pint of juice, mix juice and sugar dissolving over slow heat. When dissolved, bring to the boil, boil hard for 3-5 minutes and skim with a wooden spoon. Test a little on a saucer ; allow jelly to cool; tilt saucer and, if jelly is set, it will wrinkle. Put into jars, place small circles of greaseproof paper over jelly, label, cover with jam pot covers. Store in a dry larder until required.

Glossary

Bain-marie (au) To cook at temperature just below boiling point in a bain-marie (a saucepan standing in a larger pan of simmering water). Used in the preparation of sauces, creams and food liable to spoil if cooked over direct heat. May be carried out in oven or on top of stove. A double saucepan gives similar result. Sauces and other delicate dishes may be kept hot in a bain-marie at less than simmering heats.

Blanch To whiten meats and remove strong tastes from vegetables by bringing to boil from cold water and draining before further cooking. Green vegetables should be put into boiling water and cooked for up to 1 minute.

Caramelise 1 To dissolve sugar slowly in water then boil steadily, without stirring, to a toffee-brown colour. 2 To give a thin caramel topping by dusting top of sweet with caster or icing sugar, and grilling slowly.

Compote Fresh or dried fruit poached in a syrup, usually of sugar and water.

Dredge To cover liberally with, or immerse in, sifted flour / sugar.

Infuse To sleep in liquid (not always boiling) in warm place, to draw flavour into the liquid.

Marmelade Fruit stewed and reduced until a thick, almost solid purée. Used as flan filling. Not to be confused with marmalade.

Scald 1 To plunge into boiling water for easy peeling. 2 To heat a liquid, eg. milk, to just under boiling point.

Shortening Fat which when worked into flour gives a short crisp quality to pastry / cakes. Fats with least liquid, eg. lard, vegetable fat, contain most shortening power.

Slake To mix arrowroot / cornflour with a little cold water before adding to a liquid for thickening.

Index

158